Wit and Humor from Old Cathay

Translated by Jon Kowallis

Panda Books

Panda Books
First edition 1986
Copyright 1986 by CHINESE LITERATURE
ISBN 0-8351-1333-7

Published by CHINESE LITERATURE, Beijing (37), China
Distributed by China International Book Trading Corporation
(GUOJI SHUDIAN), P.O. Box 399, Beijing, China
Printed in the People's Republic of China

CONTENTS

Translator's Preface

THE use of humor in China can be traced back to the recorded discourses of her ancient pre-Qin philosophers, dating roughly from the sixth to the third century BC, where it served as a rhetorical device similar to the parables and anecdotes that were to appear slightly later in Greco-Roman tradition. Confucius, for example, was born in 551 BC, a generation earlier than the Buddha in India, and died in 479 BC, a decade before the birth of Socrates in Greece. His were troubled times of chaos and disunion, which prompted him to discourse upon the principles of good government, in the hope that China's feudal lords and princes might heed him. In his discourses, and those of his successor Mencius (ca 372-289 BC), humorous anecdotes served at times to illustrate a concept, prove a point, or clinch an argument. Likewise, the philosophers of rival schools such as Zhuangzi (ca 369-288 BC), Liezi (fourth century BC), Han Fei (ca 280-233 BC), and Yanzi (fl 500 BC?) also employed humorous stories to explicate their doctrines, deflate their opponents, or to touch upon some ineffable and mystic truth.

In the *Shi Ji* (Records of the Historian), a voluminous work by Sima Qian (ca 145-80 BC), which became a model for much of subsequent Chinese historiography, the foremost historian did not neglect to include a special section entitled *Huaji Liezhuan* or "Biographies of the Comics", which recounts humorous remarks (mostly didactic in nature) by some of the most celebrated wags of ancient China like Chunyu Kun and Dongfang Shuo. They employed facetious comparisons, zany outbursts, and eccentric behavior to remonstrate against everything from excesses at court to errors or misjudgments in state-to-state diplomacy, becoming valued courtiers and advisers to kings, something like the court jesters in medieval Europe, but at a higher and more respected level.

From all this it might appear that humor has been held in high regard by the Chinese since the earliest of times and occupies a primary place in their literature. But it has also been argued that none of this is humor for humor's sake, since it all serves to prove a point and that the Chinese, an intensely "practical" people, for millennia under the tutelage of moralistic monarchies and stuffy scholar-bureaucrats, have long since consigned purely humorous writings to categories the rough equivalent of "smut" in the West, approving officially of nothing other than dry, formal essays and highly stylized verse, and that the most popular current term for humor in their language, *youmo*, had to be borrowed from the West for want of a similar concept in their own culture. The prominent modern writer Lu Xun (1881-1936) was fond of the position that since nothing humorous was to be found in the Chinese situation, there could be nothing to laugh at. Nevertheless, there are many instances of humor in Lu Xun's own works, be it satiric, sarcastic, "black", or otherwise, all of which serve to entertain as well as to shed light on the darker side of human character, etc. In fact, in his *Zhongguo Xiaoshuo Shi Lüe* (Brief History of Chinese Fiction),

Lu Xun became one of the first modern scholars to chronicle, albeit briefly, the earliest anthologies in China specifically devoted to humor.

The first of these, entitled *Xiao Lin* (A Forest of Jokes), was a three *juan* compilation by Handan Chun (fl ca 221 AD), a man from Yingchuan who lived during the Later Han and Wei eras (25-220 AD; 220-265 AD). Although the original compilation is no longer extant, twenty or so of its extracts have been preserved in the *Taiping Imperial Encyclopedia* and in the *Taiping Miscellany,* giving us an idea of what they were like. Two of them follow, both from the *Miscellany.*

In the land of Lu* there was once a man who tried to enter a city gate while carrying a long pole. If held vertically, the pole was too high to make it under the gate; if held horizontally, the gate was too narrow to allow him to advance. Unable to think of any other way to get it through, the man was presently approached by an elderly gentleman, who announced: "Though sage I be none, I have witnessed many things in my life-time. Pray, couldst thou not saw thine staff in half and then clear the limits of the portal with it in hand?" The man then acted accordingly and split his own pole in two!

A and B came to blows with one another, in the course of which A bit off B's nose. When the case had been brought to court and the magistrate

---

* Now in Shandong Province.

was about to pronounce a verdict, A insisted that B had bitten off his *own* nose.

The magistrate shot back: "A man's nose is above his mouth, how could he reach it to bite it off?"

" 'Twas simple!" responded A. "He merely climbed upon a bed to do so!"

The first condemns the gullibility of its anti-hero more so than his lack of geometric common sense, and the second is a parody of attempts at rationalization, as well as mockery of the yamen court scenario (a frequent target of old Chinese jokes). As such, they have a universal as well as regional appeal, and are not limited to the more abusive forms which often characterized medieval humor.

This is not to argue that China has been blissfully free of stereotypes in her humor; indeed; in many of the anecdotes that follow in this book, we get the impression it is almost pre-supposed that every cook is a thief, every monk a hypocrite, every doctor a charlatan, every official a tyrant, every drinker a sot, every in-law a boor, every host a miser, and every guest of a miser a hideous glutton. But rather than mocking an isolated or disadvantaged group in order to enforce the socialization of their behavior (as do a good number of ethnic jokes in the West), the Chinese humor of stereotypes attempts to exhort even those who are themselves the first to admit, even to boast of their excesses, to consider the feelings and pains of others, at least for the moment. From this point of view, it may be seen as embodying a populist humanitarian ethos, and a democratic anti-authoritarian strain, tempered of course by the customs and morality of its day.

The actual origins of this sort of humor promise to be the subject of debate for a long time to come. Does it spring from the mouths of the people as a spontaneous reaction to social conditions? Or is it merely a means by which a disaffected group of literati have, throughout the centuries, recorded their grievances and effected a form of vengeance upon those whose success or blissful ignorance once taunted them? Perhaps the truth lies somewhere between the two, perhaps it lies elsewhere. Nevertheless, Chinese joke collections have obviously been the result of cumulative effort over the centuries, as is evident from the large incidence of borrowing from predecessors and re-telling old jokes with new narrative details, the style of the oldest generally being more spartan and devoid of padding, as was characteristic of the old literary language. By the Ming (1368-1644) and Qing (1644-1911) dynasties, the language of the jokes approaches the vernacular and thus becomes more wordy, though the stylistic differences may not be felt in English translation.

The selections in this book have been gleaned from over thirty different sources, starting with the *Taiping Miscellany* (981 AD), which was compiled during the Song dynasty, but contains humor materials as old as the Later Han (which I have mentioned before in connection with Handan Chun, who lived during the second and third centuries AD) and the Sui dynasty* (the

---

* AD 581-618.

Qi Yan Lu or *Record of Glee,* attributed to Hou Bai).*
In the Song dynasty (920-1279), a number of humor
anthologies were compiled: the *Xuan Qu Lu*
(Record of Jocundity) by Lü Juren (1084-1145), the *Xie
Shi* or *History of Humor* by Shen Shu, the *Kai Yan
Lu* (Record of Merriment) by Zhou Wenqi, the *Shan
Xue Ji* or *Book of Banter* by Tian He Zi, and the *Aizi
Zashuo* or *Tales of Master Ai,* attributed to the famous
Song poet Su Dongpo (1036-1101). The Yuan
(1271-1368) and Ming (1368-1644) dynasties saw more
than ten such collections published, many of which
draw on older sources or on events of the day. The
most impressive of these are the *Xiao Zan* (In Praise
of Laughter) by Zhao Nanxing and the *Xiao Fu* (A
Treasure-house of Laughter), compiled by Feng Menglong (1574-1646), both of the Ming. These two collections are liberally represented here, along with a number of their predecessors. By Qing times (1644-1911),
there were *Xiao Dao* (Rolling in Laughter), compiled
by the Ming loyalist Chen Gaomo, and the more low-
brow *Xiao De Hao* (A Good Laugh) done by Shi Chengjin of Yangzhou, also of the early years of the Qing
era. Other Qing materials include the *Xi Tan Lu* (Record of Jovial Talk), the *Xin Juan Xiao Lin Guang Ji*
(New Expanded Forest of Laughter), and the *Xiao Lin
Guang Ji* (Expanded Forest of Laughter), the last of
which was published in 1899, only a year before the
Boxer Rising and twelve years before the fall of the last
dynasty as a result of the 1911 Revolution.

---

* Hou Bai died during the reign of the first Sui emperor. A
number of jokes from the anthology attributed to him are presented
here.

In short, we have attempted here to provide the contemporary reader with a taste, be it balanced or otherwise, of classical Chinese humor from the last thousand years or so. Like much medieval humor in the West, it tends at times toward the bawdy and the grotesque, and is more than often insensitive. But once its limitations are recognized, it should prove a source of enjoyment to the general reader, as well as the student of folklore and the so-called "lesser tradition" in old China.

So far as translation is capable of preserving humor, I have endeavored to remain as close to the original texts as possible. These are not re-writes, nor are they re-adaptations, but only in that sense should they be regarded as "plain and literal translation". At times it has been necessary to re-phrase a line or two in order to make it conform to the style in which jokes are normally rendered in English, and some "punch lines" had to be altered slightly. Nevertheless, I am confident that their spirit has remained the same as in the original Chinese and therefore ask the reader's indulgence in this.

Jon Kowallis

from the **Record of Glee,** attributed to Hou Bai, Sui
dynasty

Poor Memory

LIU Zhen, the magistrate of Luoyang, was known for
his poor memory. A certain criminal was sentenced to
punishment by flogging, and upon learning the particu-
lars of the case, Liu became so indignant that he decided to execute the flogging himself. The criminal was
ordered to take off his robe and assume the position
for the lash, but he waited for some time without feeling its cut. It so happened that a visitor had just arrived
to see the magistrate and they went off to chat in the
reception room. As wintry weather prevailed at the
time, the criminal lying prostrated on the ground outside was unable to stand the bitter cold, so he took
down a coat that was hanging on a rafter to be aired
and covered himself with it.

Presently, the magistrate came out of the reception
room to cordially see his visitor off at the gate. On
noticing a figure in a coat groveling on the ground, he
shouted: "What are you here for? To catch lice?" The
criminal then hastened to leave the premises and no
further mention was ever made of the case.

Tailed Beans

DURING the Sui, a doltish carter was transporting a load of black beans to the capital for sale. His cart overturned at Batou and its cargo plunged into a body of water. The carter then abandoned the shipment and hastened back to his native place to obtain help in dredging the sacks of beans out of the water.

But while he was away the villagers in the locale salvaged the sacks and took them away. So upon his return, the driver could but dredge up schools of tadpoles. Taking them for beansprouts, he tried to grasp hold of them, but the tadpoles shot away the instant his hands approached. Heaving a long sigh, he called to them, saying: "Beans, o errant beans, why think thee a mere tail conceals thee from thy rightful master?"

Buying a Slave

A simpleton from Dongzishang Village in the district of Huxian was sent by his aged father to the market, there to buy a slave. The father instructed him beforehand: "It is said that in Chang'an, when they deal in quality slaves, the fact that the slave is up for sale is always concealed from him, and he is kept in some other place until the price and details have all been concluded."

Arriving at the market, the son chanced to step before a mirror. In the mirror he saw a young and able-bodied man. Pointing at the mirror, he asked its seller: "How much do you expect to get for this slave?" Seeing the young man's ignorance, the wily seller gibed: "*This* slave is worth ten thousand cash, easily!"

The young man then paid him that amount of money for the mirror and brought it home with him. On his return home, however, his father met him at the gate and demanded: "Where is the slave that you were to have brought?" "Right here," replied the son, drawing the mirror out from under his coat and presenting it to his father.

But the father saw in it the figure of an old man with hair and eyebrows white and a dark wrinkled face. In a fit of anger, he made ready to beat his son, yelling: "How could you spend ten thousand cash on this old man of a slave?" and wielded his walking stick menacingly at the lad.

In a great fright, the son called out for his mother, who rushed in with her young daughter in her arms, came forward and asked to have a look at the slave. She too became instantly infuriated, but this time at her husband, saying: "You old idiot, my son spent only ten thousand cash and got two slaves for it — one maid and her daughter, too! And *you* call *that* extravagant!"

Cravings

THERE was once a monk who developed a sudden craving for steamed wheat-flour cakes, so he ordered several dozen of them made outside his temple. He then bought himself a bottle of honey and retired to his quarters in the temple to partake of the cakes alone. What he could not finish, he hid in an alms bowl, which he placed, together with the bottle of honey, underneath his bed and directed the acolytes to make sure that none of it disappeared while he was gone, adding that the bottle was filled with a type of poison that would cause instantaneous death if consumed.

Soon afterward, the monk left his quarters and during his absence his disciples took nearly all the cakes, spread them with honey, and devoured them. On his return, the monk only found two left and not a drop of honey in the bottle. The indignant monk demanded to know why they had eaten his cakes and honey. A disciple replied: "We took them, master, because we could not resist their delectable aroma. But once we had eaten them, out of fear of your wrath, we decided to take the poison and seek deliverance in the immediate death you promised; yet we live still!"

The monk then kept ranting on about how could they have possibly eaten so many of the cakes, so two of his disciples quickly removed the remaining two, and popped them into their mouths, saying: "*This* is how it was done, master!"

The Signal of the Bell

A monk of quite advanced years continued to chant together with his younger brethren every day in the same prayer hall before the statue of the Buddha, even though he often fell short of breath and his throat became parched easily. Because of this he always needed a cup of warm wine nearby as a convenient antidote.

For this purpose he had made arrangements for the wine to be warmed at a certain time in the kitchen and, to avoid disturbing the other monks in their chanting, he instructed the acolytes to commence to warm the wine whenever they heard the "ding, ding, ding" sound of a brass bell at a certain point in the ritual. This procedure was followed for several days without any complications.

But the acolytes neglected their duties one day as they fooled around among themselves and brought the wine in cold. When the monk noticed this, he scolded them, saying: "Why did you not listen for the sound of the bell?" At that, the disciples insisted: "But we did, master! It went 'ding-dong, ding-dong' this time and we had been instructed to warm the wine only when it went 'ding, ding, ding'!"

The old master laughed and refrained from reproving them further.

Equal Work

A licentiate preparing to sit for the official examinations was struck by a bout of melancholia. In an attempt to console him, his wife observed one day that "preparation for those 'eight-legged' essays is as trying as childbirth!"

"Women have the easier job!" he shot back. "How so?" queried the wife. "You have everything inside already!" he sighed.

A Revelation

WHILST partaking of vegetarian fare, a man suddenly noticed a distinct flavor of mutton. He was later told by a deity in a dream: "That vegetable patch must have been invaded by sheep."

Faulty Arrows

DENG Xuanting, a man of the Tang era, used to practice archery together with Xie You, who thought himself a great archer, but who one day missed the target time and again, Xie then insisted: " 'Tis obviously the quality of arrow, for I have never shot like this before." "But the shooting is done by the archer," responded his partner, "and not by the arrows!"

The Doctrine of Ultimate Causes

A Shandong man married a girl from Puzhou, where many people are victims of goiter. His mother-in-law had a big one.

Several months after the wedding, the bride's family developed a suspicion that this new son-in-law was not treating his wife well. One day the father-in-law held a feast attended by a large number of his own relatives. At the gathering the old man decided to grill his son-in-law publicly, saying:

"Tell us, my good young man, since you have studied in Shandong, why the crane should sing."

"Nature wills it!" replied the son-in-law.

"And how is it that the pine and cypress are green in winter?"

"Nature causes it to be so," he repeated.

"Then why is it that the wayside trees have knots on their trunks?"

"That, too, is due to nature."

The old man then adjudicated to the crowd: "This fine fellow is completely ignorant of the most basic principles. Pray, tell me why did he waste his youth drifting about Shandong?" Then his father-in-law continued to mock him, saying: "The crane can sing as it does because it has a deep throat due to the length of the neck; the pine and cypress trees are green in winter because they are firm of substance, and solid at the core; the wayside trees have knots on their trunks because they have been hit by passing carts over the course of the years. How can all these phenomena be attributed to nature alone?"

The son-in-law replied: "Am I to be permitted to speak frankly for a moment?" "Of course," responded the father-in-law.

"Does the croaking of a frog arise from a long neck?" proceeded his son-in-law. "The bamboo is also green in winter. Is that due to its solid substance and empty core? Was that goiter on your wife's neck caused by a collision with a cart?"

The old man was dumbstruck with humiliation.

The Stutterer

IN the Sui dynasty there was a man who was quite sharp, but had a bit of a stutter. Yang Su, in his idle moments, would frequently invite him over for a chat to amuse himself. Once, close to the new year, when he was free, Yang had him in to sit a while and posed the question: "Suppose there were a pit ten feet deep and ten feet in circumference. If you fell into the pit, how would you get out?"

After bowing his head in deep thought for a good

while, the man ventured to ask: "Might there be a ladder in this pit?"

"Of course not!" Yang shot back at him. "If there were a ladder the question would be meaningless."

— "Is it in da-, da-, daylight, or at ni- ni- night?" he queried further.

— "The question is how to get out of the pit. Whether it is daytime or night is immaterial," replied Yang.

"If it were not night time and if I were not blind, pray, how could I fa-, fa-, fall into the pit in the fi-, fi-, first place?" retorted the luminary.

Yang burst into laughter.

Further on into their conversation, Yang asked: "Suppose you were assigned to the post of commander in a small city defended by a garrison of less than a thousand soldiers and if the grain supply could last but several days, what would you do in the event that the city were besieged by a force of several tens of thousands?" He then quickly added: "Your opinion is sought only because there could be no reinforcements forthcoming."

Raising his head, the wit replied: "In the ca-, ca-, case you have de-, de-, described, the best and inevitable solution is to surrender!"

Yang continued: "You are obviously a capable man and an acknowledged authority on many subjects. If a member of your family were bitten by a snake today and needed medical treatment, what would you do?" Our stuttering pundit responded: "A cure may be ef-, ef-, effected by rubbing the snakebite with melting snow to be gathered from the bottom of the southern exposure of a wall on the fifth day of the fifth lunar month."

"But," Yang chimed in, "how can one expect to find snow in the fifth month?"

" 'Tis true one cannot expect snowfall in the fifth month," he replied, "but where would one fi-, fi-, find a snake no-, no-, now when you speak, for it is in the mi-, mi-, middle of winter?"

After a hearty laugh, Yang saw his guest on his way.

A Connoisseur of Watchdogs

HOU Bai was not originally a well-known figure in his native district, so when a new magistrate arrived from another province and he went to the latter's office to pay his respects, boasting to the chief attendant that within a short time he could have the magistrate barking like a dog, the attendant was naturally skeptical and entered into a wager with Hou Bai on the proposition, the loser having to treat the winner to a goodly feast subsequent to the arranged audience. Hou was then allowed to enter, whilst the attendant remained directly outside the portals, waiting to hear.

At the audience the magistrate asked: "To what cause owe I the honor of this visit?"

Hou Bai replied: "At Your Excellency's arrival, your humble subjects beg to seek Your Excellency's instruction on some abnormal developments in the locale. Prior to Your Excellency's assumption of office, the locale has been plagued for quite some time now by banditry, so a directive was issued for the residents to keep dogs, and the barking of these dogs has served until now as our only means to ward off these hoodlums!"

"If that is so," observed the magistrate in haste, "then I, too, should keep barking dogs in my home. How, pray tell, since I am from out of town, shall I go about locating the best watchdogs in these parts?"

"I have in my house a number of dogs, the bark of which is quite different from ordinary ones," replied Hou.

"How so?" the distraught magistrate queried.

Hou replied: "Their bark goes 'Yow! Yow!'"

"What?" cried the magistrate. "You have not the iota of an idea of the bark of a good watchdog! It should sound more like 'How! How!' Yowling dogs are utterly useless for such a purpose."

On hearing the magistrate's reply, all the minor attendants began to snicker up their sleeves at the way in which Hou Bai had won his wager.

from the **Record of Humorous Chatter,** compiled by
Zhu Kui, Tang dynasty

On Sunning

ON the seventh day of the seventh lunar month Hao
Long chose to lie down in the sun. When someone asked
what he was doing,* he replied: "As with books, a
man needs an occasional sunning to avoid mildew."

---

* In agrarian China, the suntan has been slow in being adopted
as an institution of beauty, unlike in the post-industrial West, where
it is commonly identified with luxury and leisure. Peasants all
worked in the sun, the leisured classes avoided its rays.

from **Tales of Master Ai,** ascribed to Su Dongpo, but probably of somewhat later origin

The Use of the Bell

YINGQIU, who was a bit slow, often found it difficult to grasp whys and wherefores of things. One day he visited Master Ai and asked: "Why is it that bells are often attached to the shaft of a cart or fastened around the neck of a camel?"

Master Ai replied: "Carts and camels are of great size. Both are means of transport employed frequently at night. Since on a narrow path it is hard to dodge either one coming from the opposite direction, the sound of bells is a warning for travelers to make way."

Yingqiu again asked: "Bells are also hung from a pagoda. Do you mean that pagodas also travel at night and the bells serve as a warning to pedestrians?"

The master chided: "How can you be out of tune with the principle of things to such an extent! Birds often build nests on tall buildings with the result that these become caked with guano. For that reason, the bells are on pagodas to keep the birds away. This idea is quite different from the principle of attaching bells to a cart or camel."

Yingqiu went on: "A small bell is sometimes fastened to the tail of a sparrow hawk. Is that an indication that birds also build nests on the tails of sparrow hawks?"

With a laugh, Master Ai replied: "Wonderful! You are so idiotic. When a falcon is flying in pursuit of its prey, if it flies deep into the forest and the string attached to its feet becomes snagged on a tree, when it struggles and flutters about, the bell rings and by following the sound of the bell the falconer can trace his bird down. How could anyone construe the bell to be there to discourage nest building?"

But Yingqiu pressed on: "I often noticed mourners in a funeral procession with bell in hand, singing a dirge. Yet I hadn't the foggiest idea why. Now I understand quite well. Perhaps they might get snagged on the way by tree branches and in that case it would be easy to trace them. Still I don't know what you should fasten to a man's legs — a string or a leather rope?"

In exasperation, Master Ai could but reply: "Those attending a funeral walk before the catafalque, and as good friends of the deceased, they sound the bells to entertain the corpse!"

The Frog's Tail

WHILE at sea, Master Ai anchored for the night in the cove of an island. At night he heard the sound of weeping coming from the water, coupled with human-like voices. Listening more carefully, he overheard this conversation:

"The Dragon King has issued a decree yesterday to

the effect that all aquatic animals that have tails are to be beheaded. As I am an alligator, I weep because I am afraid of death. But thou art a frog, and hast no tail. Why weepest thou then?" Thereafter, he heard the plaintive reply: "I am indeed fortunate to have no tail at present, but the fact that I did once bear a tail as a tadpole might be recalled."

Like Father, Like Son

A wealthy man in the state of Qi was possessed of a great fortune. His second son, however, was practically an idiot, yet the father cared not enough to have him taught. One day Master Ai told the father: "Although your son is fair of face, he does not understand the ways of the world. How can you expect him to manage the affairs of your family in the future?"

Enraged, the father shot back: "My son is both clever and capable. How can you accuse him of being ignorant of the ways of the world?"

The master replied: "Then let us test him by asking whence comes the rice he eats. If he is clear about that then I have truly maligned him."

Calling his son before him, the father posed the question. The son replied with a silly laugh: "Why that's hardly difficult! It's fetched from the sack each time."

The father's expression suddenly fell and he observed: "My son is an idiot. He should have simply replied: 'From the field!'"

Master Ai commented: "Like father, like son."

Even the Gods Fear Bullies

IN the course of a trip by boat, Master Ai noticed a temple, not very high but magnificent in its ornamentations. There was a ditch in front of it. Unable to cross the ditch, someone moved an idol off of its pedestal in the temple and laid it across the ditch, enabling him to cross over. Seeing this happening, another man heaved a deep sigh and said: "How can the image of a god be treated with such disrespect?" He picked the idol up, cleaned it off with his own robe, and then restored it to its original place. He departed only after having made obeisance before it.

Soon thereafter, Master Ai overheard an imp in the temple addressing the idol: "O, great king, you are mighty enough to sit here and receive the offerings from people all over, yet you let yourself be humiliated by a foolish knave. Why not punish him for this affront by causing disasters to befall him?" But the idol replied: "Misfortune shall befall all those who henceforth offend me."

"What about the man who tramped over you and subjected you to utter humiliation?" the imp asked. "Why not place a curse on him? Why should misfortune befall future worshippers and supplicants appearing before you in reverence, *why*?" The god replied: "Since the man who desecrated my image did not have faith in me, how am I to visit disaster upon him?"

Master Ai concluded: "Indeed it is true that even the gods fear bullies."

The Old Woman's Sorrow

WHILE on a stroll Master Ai came across a white-haired woman in ragged attire who was wailing in deep sorrow. He asked: "Venerable lady, what ails you that you weep so?" "I weep for the death of my husband," replied the old woman.

Master Ai then observed: "You are quite advanced in years yourself, yet still you mourn the death of a husband. Tell me, who was he?"

The old woman replied: "Peng Zu."

"Why, Peng Zu lived to the age of 800 years! With a longevity such as his, surely there is little to regret," said the master.

The old woman sighed and replied: "Indeed, the death of my husband at the age of 800 leaves little to feel grieved about. But, there are some who are still alive at 900! *That* is what I regret!"

The Knowledge of the Carnivore

THE abode of Master Ai was surrounded by philistines from the state of Qi. One was heard to remark to another: "The nobles of Qi and I all share the same good physique, yet they are wise and I am not. Why?" The second replied: "They have meat on the table every day; hence, they are wise. We eat coarse rice and ordinary fare most of the time. Hence, we are short of wisdom."

The first then ventured: "I have just earned several thousand cash through the sale of grain and can afford to supply us both with a daily ration of meat. So let us see what comes of it."

Several days later, the two were overheard in conversation once again: "Since I first partook of meat," said one, "I have become an authority on everything. I am not only wise but can also fathom the principles behind all things." The other chimed in an agreement.

Afterwards, they began to pontificate to each other. The first held forth, saying: "I have observed that one is swift in walking if one always goes forward, but that one's feet are bound to be tripped eventually if one keeps walking backward!"

And the second made the pronouncement: "I have noticed the apertures of people's nostrils point downward, for if these were the other way round, they might be filled by water in the event of rain!"

Master Ai could but sigh and observe: "Such is the knowledge of the carnivore!"

from **A Compilation of Humor,** Song or Ming
dynasty

Contrary to the Needs of the Times

ONE day, after withdrawing from the court, Su
Dongpo went to meal. Afterwards he rubbed his
belly and strolled along slowly. Looking toward his
attendants, he said, pointing at his stomach, "Tell me,
what have I in here?" A slave girl piped up at once:
"It is full of literary works, master!" But Dongpo did
not approve of this answer. Another said: "My Lord's
belly is swollen with the mechanism of creation!"
Dongpo did not agree with that either. Then he saun-
tered over to his favorite maid Zhaoyun, who volunteered: "A court official must have a belly full of
whatever is out of keeping with the needs of the times."

Dongpo was convulsed in laughter.

from **Record of Jocundity,** a Song collection by Lü Juren

Am I a Ghost?

DUKE Sima Guang lived an idle life at Luoyang. During the Lantern Festival, his wife wished to go out into the streets to see the lanterns. The duke challenged her request, saying: "We have lanterns at home, why take the trouble of going outside to view them?" "I wish to see the people on the night streets!" replied the duchess.

— "Am I a ghost?" asked the duke.

from **Record of Merriment,** a Song collection by Zhou Wenqi

Thievery

MASTER Yan was sent to the state of Chu as an emissary. Learning of his talent at argument, the King of Chu wished to create an opportunity to challenge him. At their first audience, the king secretly ordered his men to lead a bound convict before the court; he then demanded to know the identity of the man. His attendants replied simply: "A man of Qi." The king further inquired as to the nature of the crime he had committed, and his men shouted: "Thievery, sire!"

Looking directly at Master Yan, the king asked: "Is it true that men of Qi are fond of thievery?" — "Your Majesty knows quite well," replied the master, "that the orange is grown south of the Yangzi, but north of the river the plant grows trifoliate. This is explained by the differences in the water and the soil. This man seems never to have committed thievery while in Qi, but has turned to it in Chu. Could this then not be ascribed to the customs and influences he has met in Chu?"

The king and his ministers were sore ashamed, and no reply was forthcoming.

Confidence in the Measurement

IN the state of Zheng, a man who wished to purchase a pair of shoes first measured his feet with a piece of string. On arriving at a shoe stall in the market, however, he discovered he had forgotten to bring the measurements with him. With a pair of shoes already in hand, he exclaimed: "Oh no! I have forgotten my measurements at home," dropped the shoes and returned home to fetch the string with which he had measured his size.

On his return to the market, the stalls had already closed. A man then queried: "Why didn't you just try on the shoes?"

— "Because I have more confidence in a measurement than in myself," the man replied.

from the **Jichuan Xiao Lin,** prob. a Song compilation
by Master Lu (?)

A Fiery Temper

A group of people were sitting around a stove on a
wintry day when one man of phlegmatic temperament
suddenly announced to one of those present: "I have
noticed something going on for some time now, but
have hesitated to tell you, since I know you are hot-
tempered. Yet should I fail to inform you before long,
I fear you may sustain serious bodily injury. Shall I
go ahead and tell you or not?"

"Well, be out with it, man!" the hot-tempered fellow
exclaimed. Consequently, the first man shouted: "Your
robe is on fire, sir!" The victim of the blaze immediately ripped off his own robe and stamped out the
flames. Enraged, he cursed the other, saying: "Since
you already knew for some time that my clothing was
burning, why the devil didn't you tell me earlier?"
"You see!" the first man chortled. "Just as I have
said, I knew you'd get angry no matter what I did!"

from **Applause Winners,** a Song compilation, authorship contested

Exchange Books for Bronzes

ZHANG Wenqian once recounted that: "Of late, book publishing has been flourishing, but the learned have to pay for the books themselves. A certain scholar converted all his belongings into thousands of cash with which to buy books. On his way to the capital with them, he chanced to meet another scholar who glanced over his new acquisitions. The latter appraised these books highly and wished to buy them, but lacked the funds to pay for them, but he happened to have a collection of bronze wares at home and decided to first dispose of them in order to pay for the books. But the scholar with the books happened to fancy antique bronzes, and so he was overjoyed by a chance at them, remarking: 'You need not sell them, for I wish to keep all your pieces and shall give you my books in exchange.' He then exchanged all his books for the dozens of bronzes and returned home, surprising his wife with the quickness of his return from the capital. Looking at his baggage, she noticed two or three cloth sacks full of articles that made a sort of clanging. When she learned of the exchange, his wife reviled him, saying: 'You have swapped articles, alright, but when will you be able to put food on the table?' 'By exchanging these bronzes for books,' he replied, 'neither is the other man nearer to his meals!'

"And so it is often said: 'People are the cause of their own demise.' "

Poetry Showing Intimate Feeling

LI Tingyan once submitted a hundred-rhyme poem to a superior official. The poem contained the following lines: "My younger brother died south of the Yangzi. My elder brother perished north of the Great Wall." In an attempt at showing sympathy, the official remarked: "It is above and beyond the expectations of normal service that your family has suffered so greatly!"

But Tingyan suddenly replied: "Why, this didn't actually occur at all! It is merely a literary device to indicate the intimate feeling between relatives."

The official, bursting out in laughter, accepted the poem.

Tears from the Forehead

AN Hongjian had a knack for joking, but also a reputation for being henpecked. When his father-in-law died, he wept all the way through the funeral procession. His wife, who kept strict supervision on his behavior, called him on the carpet and scolded him behind the scenes, saying: "Why is it that I saw no tears?" His wife further admonished: "At the burial when you are beside the coffin you should show your tears." He agreed to do so.

Complying with his wife's directive, he put on his forehead a pile of wet paper wrapped in a big handkerchief, and then proceeded to kowtow, knocking his head with great force on the ground, while all the time wailing loudly. Thereafter, his wife called him in again. Looking at his forehead, she said in a tone of surprise: "Tears should pour from the eyes, why are *yours* dropping from your forehead?" Hongjian replied: "Haven't you ever heard it said that since the beginning of time, water has always flowed downhill from the highest point?"*

Cursive Writing

PRIME Minister Zhang was fond of writing in the cursive style, but this was ridiculed by his peers in officialdom. One day, he wrote an essay and the paper was full of bold strokes, looking like flying dragons and snakes. He then urged his nephew to copy it. But

---

* Literally, from the plateaus (or "high and level places", referring to the forehead here, as opposed to the eyes).

the youngster hesitated as it was impossible for him to identify the characters. Holding up the sheet with the cursive characters on it, he asked: "What do these characters say?"

The Prime Minister glanced at them again for a while, but he, too, was unable to make them out. He then chided his nephew, saying: "Why didn't you ask me sooner? Now I have forgotten what I wrote!"

An Official's Hat on a Monk's Head

ZHANG Yi, a master at poetry, was assigned to the post of magistrate of Chengdu. Great Master Wen Jian, a bald and bare-headed monk, was a respected figure among the people in central Sichuan. One day, the monk paid a visit to the magistrate. Before he was received, he was sent to wait in the reception room together with Zhang Tangfu, an official from Huayang. At one point, Tangfu took off his official hat to scratch his head. As the great master was sitting next to him, he placed the hat on the head of the monk, an act deemed highly disrespectful to a holy man. The monk was outraged and began to rave at Tangfu.

At this juncture, the magistrate appeared. As he was taking his seat he said to himself: "This monk was never any acquaintance of that official, so what is he doing wearing the official's hat?" He then asked what was going on.

Tangfu volunteered: "As my head was itching, I had to remove my hat, and, finding no place to put it, I placed it on the idle head of the great master for a second. How was I to know he would be taken aback and blow up like this?"

The magistrate could do nothing but laugh at the situation.

The Significance of Officialdom

AFTER his voluntary surrender, Zheng Guang, a pirate operating off the coast of Fujian, was to be given an official post.* When a superior instructed him to write a poem, Zheng replied with a doggerel: "No matter whether they are civil or military officials they are all the same. The officials assumed their posts before becoming thieves, but I, Zheng Guang, was a thief before becoming an official."

---

* In return for surrendering.

from the **Miscellany of the Scholars,** Yuan dynasty;
ascribed to Chen Yuanjing of the Song

Antiquarianism

A scholar of the Qing dynasty, who was fond of antiques, would stop at no price to obtain them. One day,
a man appeared at his gate, hauling a seedy mattress,
and said: "In the past Duke Ai of the state of Lu presented this mattress to Confucius. This was the very mattress slept on by the great sage!" The scholar, greatly
pleased by such a rare find, obtained it at the cost of a
tract of fertile land he owned beyond the outer city
wall.

Later, another man appeared, selling an old walking
stick, which he claimed to have been "the cane used by
King Tai of the Zhou dynasty as he was on his way
to Bin in order to escape the barbarian invaders from
the north". "By the way," he added, "this stick is several hundred years older than that mattress of Confucius. What price can you offer?" The scholar exhausted
his family savings paying the man.

Thereafter, another man came to the house with a
rotten wooden bowl and said: "Neither your mattress
nor your stick can be called antiques by comparison with
this treasure. It was made during the days of Tyrant
Jie, much earlier than the Zhou dynasty." Considering

that this was a product of an even earlier era, he gave up his house in order to pay for it.

In exchange for the three antiques now in his possession, he had given up his arable land, his home, and exhausted his savings. Nothing remained for his subsistence. Nevertheless, he refused to think of trying to dispose of the three articles. Hence, he slept on Duke Ai's mattress, leaned on King Tai's stick and used Tyrant Jie's bowl as he went begging in the streets.

Three Brothers at Loggerheads

THERE were once three brothers in a family who did not get along. One day, they met and tried to reach an accord. "We are only three," they resolved, "so from now on, we should live in harmony. The first person to be contentious is to be fined three thousand cash by the others."

Soon afterwards, the elder brother announced: "Last night the well at the intersection was stolen by someone from the other end of the block." The younger brother chimed in: "No wonder the street was full of water after midnight and people were in an uproar!" But the third brother challenged: "That's absurd! How could anyone steal a well!"

The elder brother immediately censured him, saying: "There you go — the first one to be contentious! You will be fined three thousand cash." The third brother then returned home to fetch the money, but was questioned by his wife as to the purpose of taking so much, whereupon he told the whole story to her. On hearing it, she suggested: "You just go to bed. Let me take the money over to that elder brother of yours!"

Arriving at her brother-in-law's house, she told him: "Your younger brother felt acute pains in the abdomen when he returned home and in the wee hours of the morning gave birth to a son. Hence, he could not come in person and as he is confined to bed, he sent me here to pay the money in his stead."

The elder brother blurted out: "Why, that's preposterous! Who would believe for a moment that a man could give birth to a baby!"

His sister-in-law then replied: "Well, since you are being so contentious yourself, we shall just have to retain the money to pay back the fine you owe for your own behavior."

The Dragon King's Feast

DURING the Qin era, two brothers were obsessed with wild talk, trying to hoodwink each other into believing anything. One day, the elder brother observed: "We two have become addicted to groundless talk; we should take a bath in the stream in front of our home to wash away this perverse obsession." The younger brother agreed.

The elder then secretly took a piece of dried meat in hand, removed his clothes, and dove into the water.

After a short time, he resurfaced and, coming ashore, got dressed again, all the while carrying himself in a most affected way and conspicuously eating of the dried meat.

The younger then asked: "Where did that hunk of dried meat come from?" And the elder replied: "The Dragon King was holding a feast in the depths. Seeing that I had come swimming in his realm to wash away my old ways, he invited me to partake of the divine table. This meat is delicious! It must be dragon liver."

The younger brother, on hearing this, lost no time in stripping off his raiments and hurled himself into the water. But as he dove with such fury, his head was injured on a hidden rock. He then shot up out of the water, bleeding profusely from the head. The elder brother queried: "How came you to injure your head thus?"

"The Dragon King took exception to my later arrival and rapped me on the head with a drumstick a number of times as punishment. It was awful!" he replied.

A Guest's Retort

ONCE upon a time a man made a long stay at his father-in-law's house and refused to leave. Finally, the father-in-law told him: "Since you came from afar, we have butchered every last chicken to feed you. Now let there be no complaint if we have nothing further to offer!" He hoped the son-in-law could take a hint.

But the son-in-law replied: "You need not worry. When I first came I noticed a flock of fat deer grazing in the hills nearby here. If we can catch and cook just one, it will provide meals for many days to come."

The father-in-law retorted: "Yes, the deer were there when you first arrived, but that was over a month ago. They must have moved on by now."

But his son-in-law ruminated: "They haven't gone anyplace. The reason they were there was that good things were available to eat there, and nobody's going to quit a place where he's fed!"

The Corrupt Are Devious

A civil official named Zhou of the *tongpan* rank was accused of corruption, subjected to impeachment and demoted to be a magistrate. When he came to his new post, the officer under him, knowing of the magistrate's proclivities, had a silver doll made, weighing a catty, and placed it on a table in an antechamber of Zhou's home, telling the magistrate: "My brother will be waiting to see you in your antechamber." Zhou then went in and collected the silver doll.

Some days later, the officer, expecting a decision on his case, went in and begged the magistrate for a favor "on behalf of my brother". But the magistrate replied: "Your brother would appear to be quite indifferent to the matter, since it seems he has failed to come more often!"

from **Addendum to the Tales of Master Ai,** ascribed to Lu Zhou, Ming dynasty

Punishing a Grandson

MASTER Ai had a grandson. At the age of ten, the boy had become very lazy in his studies. Even thrashings with a rod failed to make him mend his ways. He was the only son in the family and his father was always afraid that the child might not be able to withstand a flogging.

Each time his son pleaded for leniency in tears for the boy, Master Ai angrily replied: "Am I wrong to want to educate my grandson?" and then flogged the child even more forcefully. The boy's father could do nothing to intervene.

One day, when it was snowing, the grandson was out playing in the snow when he was to have been studying. On discovering this, Master Ai stripped him and made him kneel in the snow, shivering, while he awaited his punishment. The son dared not say anything, but stripped himself naked also, kneeling down by the side of his offspring.

Master Ai exclaimed: "Your son is about to be punished for his wrongdoings, all well and good; but what are *you* doing kneeling in the snow beside him?" The boy's father replied: "*You* are freezing *my* son to death, so *I* am freezing *yours*!"

The master laughed and spared the boy.

An Arranged Marriage

YU Ren was an old friend of Master Ai. He had a daughter two years of age. The master was anxious to have the daughter engaged to his son. Yu asked: "How old is your son?" "Four years," answered the master.

"Are you planning to engage my daughter to an old man or what?" demanded Yu in an angry tone.

Failing to appreciate the meaning of these words, Master Ai queried: "What do you mean?" Yu explained: "Your son is four years old, but my daughter is only two, or half his age. Hence if my daughter is married at 20, your son will be 40. If she is married at 25, your son will be 50. Is that old or isn't it?"

Master Ai, seeing Yu Ren's ignorance, felt it inappropriate to continue.

from **Lu Shu,** compiled by Yao Lü of the Ming

The Dwarf

A man surnamed Xing, a candidate for the imperial examinations, was quite short in stature. One day he fell victim of a robber at Fanyang. After taking all of Xing's valuables, the robber raised his axe in an attempt to kill him so as to avoid incrimination later. At this juncture, Xing admonished him, saying: "People are always deriding me as a dwarf. But minus my head, I'll be even shorter!"

The robber dropped his axe in laughter.

from A Record of the Ridiculous, compiled by Liu Yuanqing of the Ming

A Disappearing Monk

A low official of the *liyi* rank was escorting a convict monk to the frontier regions to begin serving his sentence. On the way at night, the crafty monk offered wine to the official who became drunk and fell sound asleep. He then cut the queue off the official's head and wound it around his neck before fleeing. At daybreak, the groggy official arose and could not find the monk anywhere. He then patted his head, expecting to find his queue, but discovered it wrapped around his neck instead. Greatly dismayed, he said to himself: "The monk is here, all right, but where then am I?"

How to Cook Goose

THERE was once a hunter who, spotting a wild goose in flight and about to fire an arrow, observed: "I shall fry this one once it is shot down." His brother piped in, saying: "A domestic goose tastes good fried, but a wild goose is only good roasted!"

After much quarreling, they brought their arguments

before a neighborhood elder who opined: "Cut the goose into halves, one half to be fried and the other to be roasted." But on their return to locate the goose, it had already flown far from sight.

A Blind Man's Lack of Faith

A blind man fell from a bridge spanning a dried stream. His hands held fast to the railing, believing that once he loosened his grip, he would fall into the depths. A passerby remarked: "Fear not lest you loose your grip, for there is solid ground beneath the stream."

But the blind man did not believe him, and after clinging to the railing for a long time, he became exhausted and at length, let himself drop onto the bed of the stream. Getting up, he chuckled: "Why, had I known there was solid ground beneath, I could have spared myself the ordeal!"

Locating the Spot

LONG ago, there was a man with an itch. He asked his son to scratch it for him, but the latter tried thrice, failing to locate it. He then asked his wife to do the same, but she, too, failed to locate it even after five separate tries. Disgruntled, the man complained: "A wife is supposed to have intimate knowledge of her spouse, how then does she fail me in this simple thing?" He then tried scratching with his own hand and found the spot easily.

Why could he do so so readily? Because with an itch, as with other things, a person should know himself before others.*

The Surname Wan ("ten thousand")

A rich family had been illiterate for generation after generation. Finally the patriarch of the household engaged a scholar from the state of Chu as his son's tutor. The son was taught how to write the most simple character, the pictograph for one, written with one horizontal stroke. Then he learned that the character two was written similarly, but with two strokes and the character for three with three strokes.** The boy was delighted at the end of this first lesson. Putting down the writing brush, he ran to tell his father: "I have got it, I no longer need a tutor! You shan't have to pay the cost of schooling and can send the tutor away immediately!" The father was overjoyed and paid the scholar for the day, sending him on his way.

---

* A well-known axiom.
** The others do not follow suit.

Some time later, the father wished to issue a formal invitation to a man named Wan to come over for a drink. He ordered his son to prepare an invitation card the next morning, but by late in the day, the boy was still writing. When his father, thinking the situation curious, asked him why, the boy replied in frustration: "Of all the surnames, why does he have to be called 'Ten Thousand'? Working all day, I have only been able to draw five hundred!'

from **Ridiculous Talk,** compiled by Guo Zizhang of the Ming

The Plague of Locusts

QIAN Mufu was magistrate of Rugao. For a year the district suffered both drought and a plague of locusts. But a Taixing official tried to conceal this from his superior, the chief, saying simply: "There are no locusts in my locale." Very soon swarms of locusts were all over. The prefecture chief queried the magistrate who again failed to give a satisfactory reply, answering only: "My district was originally devoid of locusts. These must have flown in from Rugao."

The magistrate of Rugao was then ordered to exterminate the locusts, and not permit them to fly into neighboring districts. When Qian Mufu received the circulating order, he added on at the end: "Locusts are a natural calamity and not the fault of any magistrate. If any have, perchance, flown out of my jurisdiction into yours, please escort them back."

from Elegant Banter, a Ming collection by Fubai-zhai Zhuren

An Idiot for a Son

IN Suzhou there dwelt a wealthy man whose son was an idiot. At the age of 30, the son was still living off his father. That year, when the father reached the age of 50, a fortune-teller predicted he would live to 80 and his son to 62. On hearing the prediction, the son burst into tears and said: "If father's life ends at 80, who will support me for my last two years?"

An Idiot for an Official

SUN Yangao, a prefectural official in a city besieged by Turks, dared not go out to perform the duties of his office. Documents requiring his perusal were passed to him through a small window. When a report was received that attackers were breaching the last defences, he locked the official mansion and entered a vault, leaving his servant with the order: "Make sure you hold onto that key! If the bandits ask, don't give it to them!"

An Idiot for a Magistrate

A native of Shandong, Ma Xin, who was magistrate of Changzhou, went by boat to an audience with a superior official. When the latter queried: "And where is your boat anchored?" Ma replied: "On the river." The superior rebuked him angrily, saying: "A load of rubbish!" But Ma replied: "Yes, we do have some of that aboard, why are you asking?"

Stumbling upon a Thief

A thief stole into the home of Yu Gong precisely at the time when Yu was entering through the front door. Being startled, the thief fled, leaving behind a fur coat which he had stolen elsewhere. Yu Gong was pleased at his new prize. With this in mind, he went out the next night, but was disappointed on his return home to find that the premises were vacant. "Why," he wondered, "did that thief fail to return with more loot?"

A Poor-Sighted Watchdog

YU Gong had eye trouble. Leaving his home to go to a doctor, he noticed his dog lying at the foot of the front steps. As he stepped over it, the dog's neck was accidentally brushed by his shoe and it nipped at him, tearing his robe at the hem.

Yu Gong related this to the doctor who jokingly said: "Your dog must be having eye trouble, too, otherwise why should it tear your robe?"

Taking his leave from the doctor, Yu thought: "Who cares if the cur did turn on me, as a watchdog it is indispensable at night." So, he prepared the medicine and offered the first dose to the dog, leaving only the dregs for himself.

Preemptive Surgery

ON hearing the views of a man afar that asserted the liver of a horse to be highly toxic and capable of poisoning people, Emperor Wu of the Han dynasty recalled: "Wen Cheng died after eating a horse's liver." These words caused great amusement to Yu Gong who observed: "This is ridiculous! While in the body of the horse it does not cause the horse to die, does it?" The stranger retorted in jest: "Well, I've never seen a horse that could reach the advanced age of a man, say one hundred, have you? This is due to its liver."

Yu Gong was suddenly won over. Since he had a horse himself, he went out and removed its liver and the horse died instantly. He then cast down his knife and remarked with a sigh: "Indeed, it must have been poisonous, since the horse could not live long after its removal. Obviously, it would have been even worse if the thing had been allowed to remain inside the body of the horse!"

Vomiting Before an Official Mansion

YU Gong was drunk. Passing before the official mansion of a counsellor, he vomited at its portals. The gatekeeper then reproached him, saying: "In your drunkenness what prompted you to commit such an impropriety as vomiting before an official mansion?" Fixing his gaze firmly upon the servant, Yu Gong said: "The gate may be yours, but it is much to my distaste." The gatekeeper, who could not keep from laughing, replied: "This gate has been here for a long time. Why should it have taken you this long to find it so distasteful?" Pointing to his mouth, Yu Gong said: "My mouth, too, has been around for years."*

---

* Obviously an issue of seniority.

A Borrowed Raiment

YU Gong, out on a rainy day, was wearing a robe borrowed from someone else when he fell on the slippery ground, injuring his arm and soiling the robe. His attendant helped him up, attempting to massage the painful bruise on his arm, but Yu Gong stopped him, saying: "Just find some water to wash the robe. You can ignore my injured arm."

When the attendant queried: "Why care about the robe but not your arm?" Yu Gong replied: "The arm, at least, is my own property and I won't have to answer to anyone for it."

Writing Paper of the Song Dynasty

YU Gong was in possession of some scrolls of writing paper produced during the Song dynasty long ago. Once a noted official of the Wu state, who was good at calligraphy and painting, visited him and remarked sarcastically: "Your paper is indeed fine, but it should be sent out to someone to be painted upon so that its fine qualities may be fully utilized to provide the utmost enjoyment to connoisseurs." "What?" retorted Yu Gong. "Do you want me to ruin my paper? Song paper was only intended to be worked by a Song master!"

Repairing a Leaking Roof

AFTER days of rain, the roof of Yu Gong's home began to leak. His bed had to be moved several times to keep from being soaked by water dripping down from the ceiling. His wife began to curse and hurl invectives, so Yu Gong hurriedly called in a roofer for repairs at seasonally great expense. The repair work at last done, good weather set in and the skies were clear for the next month. Looking at the ceiling, Yu Gong observed with a sigh: "A man of bitter fate indeed! My roof just repaired, the rain ceases. All these expenses incurred in vain!"

A Low Stool

YU Gong had a stool which was very short. Every time he went to sit upon it, he first had to place some tiles underneath its feet to raise it up. Tiring of this, he had a sudden brainstorm and ordered a servant to move the stool upstairs. However, he soon discovered that it was still as low as ever. Thereupon he proclaimed: "People all say that the second floor is higher. But that is just not the case." He then ordered his servants to demolish his top floor.

A False Alarm

IN the eighth month of the lunar calendar great waves always roared on the sea by night, disturbing the tranquility of a certain town in Shandong. During the Zhi Zheng reign period, a man named Bu Hua arrived in the locale, but dared not sleep at night because of this fearsome sound. He inquired of the sleeping servant who replied groggily: "It is but the coming of the tide." Bu Hua hurried to his wife's quarters in the inner chamber and told her: "I originally hoped to become an official of great renown, but now discover we are fated to perish together this night in a gigantic tidal wave!"

With that, he shut all the doors as tightly as possible and they all commenced a great wailing. Outside, the night watchman heard the sound and became immediately convinced that some sort of accident had occurred. He reported this to the sentries, who donned their uniforms and roused themselves to go to the rescue. Bu Hua, fearing lest the ocean should pour in, had bolted the doors and battened the hatches, and was not about to admit anybody. This forced the battalion of sentries to descend on the house, breaking in shutters and scaling walls to obtain entry.

Finally, in the inner chambers, they found Bu Hua, his wife and her servant girl perched atop the furniture and screaming their lungs out. On learning what afflicted them, the sentries stifled their laughter and returned to their quarters.

Sheer Stupidity

THE grandson of Sun Hezhai of Kunshan was a fool. Bankrupted early on, he had only two antique teapoys to his name. One day, he saw a man with a turtle passing by. He wanted to buy it but was penniless, so he exchanged one of his fine teapoys for it. The man then sold the teapoy to a neighbor for the price of two *dou* of grain. Wishing to have a pair of teapoys, the neighbor asked the man to approach Sun with another turtle in order to get hold of the other member of the set. But on being approached, Sun could only stamp his foot and moan in exasperation: "*Why* didn't you come earlier! I just chopped the other teapoy into pieces for firewood to cook the turtle!"

Pillow Talk

THE two sons of Liu Mao were both successful candidates in the imperial examinations and thus gained great prestige. The wife of the first son was going to the capital. Liu saw her to the boat and helped her aboard, grasping her hand as he did so.* On seeing this, another man burst into laughter, but Liu shot back:

---

* An obvious impropriety.

"There is nothing funny about us making such a scene! It would be much more ridiculous if she fell into the water!"

On another occasion the wife of the second son was about to depart for the capital. Her father-in-law was sick abed at the time, so he called her to his side and, patting the pillow, announced: "A man my age must take precautions against the cold. Buy me a good kerchief while in the capital, and have it sent back."

The next day, the day of her departure, many relatives gathered to bid her farewell. Liu reminded her: "Don't forget what I told you last night upon the pillow."

All present were aghast at his utterance.

An Instance of Ignorance

WANG Hao was a bit slow mentally. As a subordinate to King Wen Xuan of Qi in an expedition against the king's foes in the north, he was riding a brown horse. One day the horse was covered with frost overnight and the next morning he failed to recognize it. Wang claimed that he had lost his horse and that it was nowhere to be found. Presently, however, the sun came up and the frost was soon melted off the body of the horse, whereupon it was found tethered in the original spot where he left it. Only then did Wang proclaim: "My horse remains with us!"

Advice on Chanting

THE mother of Yongling was a devoted Buddhist, invoking the holy name of the Buddha all day long. Then one day, Yongling decided to call his mother on a pretext. The old lady answered. He then continued calling to her with great frequency. The mother grew annoyed and said: "What's this all about? Why all this yelling for me!"

Yongling replied: "Aha! You become vexed when I call your name but three or four times. Yet the Buddha is beckoned to thousands of times a day. How angry he must be!" His mother was convinced by this logic to limit her daily chanting.

A Trick

ZHU Gumin was learned but fond of joking. One day when he paid a call on Scholar Tang at his studio, the latter said: "You are known to be full of tricks. If I were sitting in a given room, could you induce me to go outdoors?" Zhu replied: "It is presently quite cold outside, so I am certain you would be unwilling to step out of doors, but if you were to stand outside this room it would be much easier for me to induce you inside; you would veritably be forced to comply with my will!"

Believing him, Scholar Tang went out of the house and said to Zhu: "Alright, how can you induce me back inside?"

Clapping his hands, Zhu replied: "But haven't I already induced you out?"

Steamed Red Sorghum

OF late a friend's mother died. One day the family chanced to eat steamed sorghum, which was of a reddish color. A local pedant felt that while in mourning it was inappropriate to have a meal with the main course in so gay a color, so he took up this point with them, pointing out that red was always indicative of happy events, such as weddings. The friend replied: "Well, I suppose all those people eating white rice every day are doing so because they are in mourning!"*

The Scion of a Venerable Old Man

A venerable old man, Jin by name, a native of Dantu, had an unworthy son, but the grandson was a successful candidate in the imperial examination. The vener-

---

* In old China, white was the color of mourning, corresponding to black in the West.

able old man often reproached his own son, but one day the man replied: "Your father was not as good as my father and thus your son was not as good as my son. How can I be regarded as unworthy?" The old man halted his reprimand and laughed heartily.

A Good Time After Death

YE Heng retired at the end of his term as prime minister. While on his sickbed he one day asked his visitors: "I am perhaps about to die, so, pray, tell me — is death a desirable state?" One among them replied: "Quite desirable, sir!" Surprised, Ye Heng continued: "How do you know?"

"If the dead were in a wretched state in the nether world," replied the visitor, "they would certainly have all come back by now, but none among their number has done so. Obviously they are happy in the other world."

This caused a roar of laughter among all present.

The Bride's Regret

OLD Master Lu lost his wife when he was old. Miss Zhu, the woman whom he then married, was so young they did not seem like a couple together. Moreover the wife sat around knitting her eyebrows every day.

Finally Lu asked: "Is it that you think I am too old?" "No," she replied. "Well, is it that you think I am an official of too low a rank?" The answer to this was also "No!" "Well, what's wrong then?" he demanded. The wife replied: "I am feeling bad about neither your age nor your rank; rather, I am resentful only of the fact that I was born too late to meet you in your prime!"

The Wine of Immortality

EMPEROR Wu Di of the Han dynasty received as tribute a wine known as the elixir of immortality. The wag Dongfang Shuo then stole this wine and drank it himself, enraging the emperor, who intended to have him executed for it. But Dongfang Shuo said: "What I have drunk is supposed to make me immortal. Therefore I cannot die. If I should die, however, that would certainly show that such wine cannot live up to its name."*

---

* In that case, both the emperor and the tributary would lose face.

from a Ming compilation, also entitled **A Forest of Jokes**, by Fubai Zhuren

A Bull Wearing a Kerchief

WHEN a rich man ordered his cowherd to dry a kerchief in the sun, the cowherd put it on the horns of a bull. While drinking at a stream the bull was startled by the unfamiliar reflection of the kerchief on the water's surface and stampeded off into the distance, leaving the cowherd to trail behind, and forcing him all along the way to ask people: "Have you seen a bull wearing a kerchief?"

The Son of an Official

A man once made the query as to who is happier — the official upon whom a high title has just been conferred or the son of a high official? Someone answered him: "An official awarded a high title must be of commensurate age, and for that reason, the son of an official is always the happier, as he can enjoy the benefits while he still has his youth."

The man then hurried away, explaining: "Well then, I should send my father off to school."

The God of Targets

WHEN a military official on an expedition was faced with an imminent debacle, he suddenly was favored with the aid of celestial soldiery, whereupon he was enabled to turn defeat into victory. The official kowtowed before the leader of these celestial troops and begged to learn his name. The deity replied: "I am the god of targets." The official asked: "What merit have I incurred that your grace should shower such favors upon me?"

"I am thankful that upon the drill ground," replied the god, "your arrows have never struck me once."

Moralists Revile One Another

TWO men met upon the road. One of them proclaimed: "You have a guilty conscience." The other retorted: "You have the guilty conscience." The first one continued: "You have no awareness of the principles of heaven!" But the second shot back: "You yourself are ignorant of such principles!"

A scholar well-versed in doctrines and principles, on hearing this exchange, said to his disciples: "Hear ye! Hearken to the sounds of scholarly discourse!" One disciple then queried: "They are but reviling one another, why does our master call this scholarly discourse?" The answer came: "When men speak of the mind and of principle, it cannot be anything but scholarly inquiry!" "If it is scholarship," ventured the student, "then wherefore all the abuse?"

"Well, any look at those engaged in debating moral issues and principles today should adequately indicate that harmony is hardly one of their concerns!" replied his teacher curtly.

Carried Off

DISCOVERING a loan to be long outstanding, an angry money-lender ordered his servant to go spy on the debtor, to apprehend and then carry him off to the house of his creditor. On the way back, the fatigued servant halted to take a rest, but his victim stammered: "Hurry up! Take me away! I owe so much money that if we stop here for too long I may be carried off by someone else."

A Fart's Escape

IN a court session someone broke wind. The presiding official demanded: "Who has caused this disturbance?

Bring the culprit before me!" But the bailiff replied: "It can't be done."

"Why not?" the official demanded. "You're deceiving me. He must be brought immediately!" The bailiff then came back with a piece of stool wrapped up in paper, telling the judge: "The main culprit has fled, Your Honor, but we have one of his relatives here!"*

Indulgences for Sale!

A scholar visiting a Buddhist temple one day was snubbed by a monk in one of the rooms in the western wing, whereupon he withdrew in a huff to the eastern wing. On seeing a monk chanting sutras there, he inquired: "On whose behalf are you repenting?"

"This is extra chanting, being performed in my spare time and may be credited to anyone, should you choose to make a donation," replied the monk.

The scholar suddenly struck the head of the holy man, who in turn whined: "How have I offended you?" The scholar replied: "Apply that knock to the credit of your bald-headed** friend over in the western wing!"

---

* Satirizing the feudal custom of arresting the relatives of persons accused of a crime.

** A term of abuse for Buddhist monks, all of whom had shaven heads.

A Monastic Haircut

A monk was having a haircut, but due to a slip of the barber's razor one of his ears was cut off. Bleeding and in great agony, the monk observed the barber pick the ear up off the ground. Holding it with both hands, the barber exclaimed: "Master, let's not do anything rash, now! You see, here is your ear, in exactly the same shape as you walked in with it."

Respects to Your Father

PRIOR to his departure for a trip, a man told his son: "If anyone comes to ask after me, you just tell him your father is away from home on some minor business and then invite the caller in for tea, if he is so disposed."

Knowing his son to be dull-witted, the father left his instructions in black and white on a piece of paper. The son kept it in his sleeve, repeating his father's injunction over and over again. But no one came for three days, and, thinking the note of no further use, the boy burnt it over a lamp. On the fourth day, however, a caller did come, wishing to see his father. The son could not find the note in the sleeve and so he simply stammered: "Gone!"

"When did it happen? — How?" the visitor inquired

with surprise. "Last night, by fire!" came the boy's reply.

A Lined Quilt

IN hot summer weather a man was sleeping with a lined quilt. Replying to someone who asked him what he needed a lined quilt for, the man said: "Because a padded one would be even hotter in this weather!"

The Money-Pouch

CARRYING silver to buy grain at a market, a man lost his money bag on the way thither. When he returned home, he attempted to excuse his loss to his wife, saying: "There was so much bustling at the market today, and it seems my pouch was not fastened too securely, so...." "You mean you have lost it!" the wife exclaimed. "Even a hero fouls up sometimes," he replied. Incredulous, the wife insisted: "Come on, where *is* the money?" "*That's* not the problem," he replied, "I *know* where the *money* is. I made sure to fix it real securely inside the pouch."

A Guest Invited to Leave for Dinner

A guest from afar sat for a long time visiting with his host. Although the courtyard was filled with ducks and chickens, the host pretended that he could not ask him to stay for dinner because there was a shortage of food. The guest then asked for a knife with which to butcher his own horse.

"How can you return home then?" the host queried. "Surely you'd be willing to *lend* me one of your fowl to ride upon," replied his indignant guest.

The Strength in Cooperation

ONCE there were two brothers who planted wheat together, sharing the labor. When their wheat was ready to harvest they discussed how to divide the yield. The elder brother told his junior: "I shall take the top half and you the lower half of the plants," leaving the younger one aghast at the inequity of this proposal. The elder then added: "If you feel something is amiss, next year you shall have the top half and I the lower." At the time of the next spring sowing, the filial younger brother naturally asked the opinion of his elder as to which type of crop to plant. "This year," replied the elder brother, "let us plant yams!"

The Decorum of Yielding Passage

ONCE when two men were on a walk together, on noticing the approach of the carriage of a notable personage, the first said to the second: "The man in the carriage is my good friend. On seeing me he would, according to the rules of decorum, be forced to alight from his vehicle as a token of respect. Therefore, as a courtesy to him, I should keep out of sight."

Unwittingly, however, the stroller proceeded to duck into the gate of this self-same notable's mansion. Taken aback at the sight of someone lurking in his portals, the celebrity demanded: "Why hide yourself within my gate in broad daylight?" He then called upon his servants to trounce and evict the man.

This scene puzzled the other man originally together with him on the street. The latter queried: "If you be anything resembling good friends, why should he have you beaten and evicted thus?" " — Such is our normal manner of jest with one another," replied the first.

Emptying the Nightstool

TWO men were both sore afraid of their spouses. One lamented to the other: "My wife has become much stricter as regards the chores lately. Now I even have to empty the nightstool!" The second raised his hands and shouted: "What an outrage. If I were you. . . ." But before he finished all that he had wanted to say, his wife's voice screamed out from behind: "If it were you what would you do now?" He then fell to his knees and pleaded: "If it were I, I'd go empty it."

The Terms of a Loan

A man persistently asked his friend for a loan, but the friend just kept refusing. Finally he told the man: "You'll just have to get down on your hands and knees if you truly wish it from me." The man promptly complied.

A bystander then rebuked him, saying: "Why are you so willing to debase yourself for a piddling amount of silver you will only have to repay later? You would never see me do that!"

The man replied: "This isn't costing me anything now. But just wait until *he* tries to collect on the loan; then *he'll* be doing the bowing and scraping."

The Broken Hairnet

A man with a broken hairnet sought to have it mended. Calling in a craftsman good at such repair work, he bent his neck and directed him to repair it while he wore it. Advised to remove it first, he protested: "But as soon as I take it off, it falls apart."

Hair as Payment

SEEING a woman sell her hair one day and receive payment in sugar, a man decided that hair could be exchanged for all types of food. And so he went out one day in the morning with a lock of his own hair. Coming across a wine shop, he ventured in. After a sumptuous breakfast, when he offered the hair in payment, the waiters burst into laughter. "Others can use hair like money," exclaimed the man in anger, "so why shouldn't it work for me?"

A long argument ensued and finally the waiters grabbed him by the hair and gave him a thorough trouncing. Afterwards, he straightened out his clothes and hair and remarked: "They refused to accept the lock of hair I had prepared, yet still wanted to snatch as much as they could grab at random off my head!"

Beancurd

A man insisted that a visitor stay for dinner, but then served only beancurd, saying: "Beancurd is my life! No other flavor is quite like it!" One day when he was himself a guest at that same visitor's house, his host took care to make sure that every dish contained some beancurd around the various portions of fish and meat. But then he noticed that his guest filled up on the fish and meat, to the exclusion of the beancurd. "Didn't you once tell me beancurd was your life?" the host asked. "Pray, why do you not partake of it today?"

"When I espy the likes of meat and fish," replied the man, "I'm willing to throw my life away!"

Vegetarianism

A cat was wearing a string of beads around its neck as a badge of vegetarianism. On seeing this, a mouse exclaimed with joy: "A vegetarian cat!" Leading its young, the mouse approached the cat to say a word of commendation, but the cat let out a loud screech and promptly pounced on them, devouring a number. Their elder escaped in haste and, tongue hanging out, gasped: "The cat nature in him must be exacerbated by vegetarianism!"

A Banquet of Humor

WHILE sleeping a man dreamt he had gone to a banquet at which operas were to be performed. Just as he was dreaming of being ushered to his seat, he was awakened by his wife. He reviled her for this disturbance but she replied: "Why not just ease your cursing and go back to sleep as quickly as possible. They are most likely not yet halfway through the opera!"

A Prized Steed

DUKE Guan possessed a piebald horse capable of galloping one thousand *li* in a single day. Zhou Cang, armed with his heavy sword, walked behind and was able to cover the same distance. Out of consideration for his needs, Duke Guan was eager to bestow a similar horse on Zhou Cang, but failed to find one of the same speed. The only one available could do but nine hundred *li* per day. This Duke Guan bought at a high price, bestowing it upon his friend.

Zhou Cang then rode out on the horse, following the duke, but fell one hundred *li* behind the first day and two hundred *li* the second. Fearing lest he might lose track of the duke's trail, but unwilling to abandon his prized mount, Zhou Cang got off the horse and tied its hooves together, hanging it from his sword as a pole over his shoulder. He then took off, carrying his load in an attempt to make up for lost time.

from **The Xue Tao History of Humor,** Ming comp. by
Jiang Yingke

Stealing the Chime

BREAKING into a house in broad daylight, a thief
stole a chime. As he was making off through the gate
with it, he ran into the owner of the house who just happened to be walking along the street toward home.
"Care for a chime, sir?" the thief at once asked the
owner. The owner replied: "No, I have one at home."
The thief then disappeared with his booty.

Only at prayer time that evening, when the owner
went to look for his chime, did he realize that the man
who had offered to sell him a chime had stolen his
own.

The Guest Who Always Overstayed
   His Welcome

A guest who always overstayed his welcome was drinking without stop one evening. Finally, feeling a bit

sated, he announced to the other guests: "Those living far away will just have to be on their way before me!" The guests, for their part, all went home except him.

Left alone with the host, he proclaimed: "Anyone else who has far to go may leave now." "But I live here," replied the host. The guest then said: "Yes, and you still have to return to your room. In my case, I shall be sleeping right here on the table!"

Telling a Lie

A young cad from Wuling was good at telling a convincing lie. On the street one day he met an old man who said: "People say you lie all the time; well, just try one on me, you young whippersnapper!" The youth replied: "There's no time to talk now. I've just heard they are draining the water from the East Lake and everybody there is busy picking up free fish from off the ground, so I'm hurrying over there to get me one, too!"

Believing his words, the old man dashed to the East Lake but found it still full on his arrival. Only then did he realize that the youth had been lying to him.

Saving One Eyebrow

WITH the New Year approaching, a young ruffian was short of money. His wife was eager to know what was to be done. The ruffian replied: "I have a secret plan!" At this juncture, a barber happened to be passing before their gate. He was promptly called in and asked to shave off the man's eyebrows. Once one eyebrow had been shaved off, the man flew into a rage, charging that no barber should ever remove someone's eyebrow completely, only make it thinner or shorter. He then threatened to drag the barber off to the yamen and press charges against him.

Reluctant to settle the matter through litigation, the barber offered 300 cash in compensation, which the ruffian accepted. With this money the couple had enough to pass the New Year Festival in the best of form. But bothered by her husband's appearance with only one eyebrow, the wife asked: "Would it not look better if both were removed?" "Have you no foresight, woman?" the ruffian replied. "This brow is to be retained for the Lantern Festival fifteen days hence! Won't we need money then?"

from **A Collection of Humor,** edited by Zhong Xing of the Ming

The Handsome Scholar

ZHANG of Songjiang, a successful candidate in the imperial examination, had a handsome deportment and was fair of face. One day he visited Fan the imperial examiner of Suzhou who was remarkably ugly. On a walk together in the market near the west gate, all the children in the vicinity began following them and staring. Zhang remarked to Fan: "They must be looking at me." "No," said Fan with the trace of a smile, "I'm afraid they are looking at me!"

from **In Praise of Laughter,** compiled by Zhao
Nanxing of the Ming

Nine Other Idiots

A villager ordered his servant to the city; no sooner had
he given the command than the servant was already on
his way. At the gate of the district magistrate's office
the magistrate was trying to collect payments on the
land tax. One of the ten neighborhood headmen did
not appear, so the servant was included with the nine
others and brought before the magistrate in their place.
For their failure to pay the land tax, the magistrate ordered a flogging of ten strokes apiece.

On the servant's return, the master asked: "What
were you up to in the city all this time?" The servant
recounted the story of the flogging. "Idiot!" laughed
the master. "What about those other nine," snapped
the servant. "Were *they* all idiots, too?"

A Felt Hat

A man was wearing a felt hat* while walking down the

---

* i.e., a hat of very warm material, not considered appropriate
summer attire.

street one hot summer day. As he came beneath the shade of a large tree, he sat down on the ground for a rest, waving his hat as a fan. There he mused to himself: "Had I not worn my felt hat today the heat would surely have killed me!"

Whipping Boy

A man was hired to receive a flogging to which another had been sentenced by an official. But it required a bribe of all the money he had been paid to take the beating before the bailiff carrying out the whipping would make the blows gentle enough to be endured.

After the chastisement was over, the "whipping boy" kowtowed to the man who had hired him to take his punishment for him and exclaimed: "Good sir, you are my true benefactor, had you not supplied ample funds, I would surely have been whipped to death!"

Telltale Shoes

A man who had been away from home returned late one night, rapping at the door to gain entry. His wife had been sleeping with another man and the two of them awakened with a start, whereupon the lover, making haste to escape through a window, left behind a pair of shoes positioned in a manner that left them jutting out from beneath the bed.

When admitted through the door by his wife, the husband chanced to notice the shoes and, thinking them suspicious, pretended not to have seen them, all the while planning to subject them to closer scrutiny on the morrow. After he had fallen asleep, however, the wife disposed of them in secret. Upon waking the next day, the husband examined a pair of shoes he found in the exact location of those he had spotted the previous night.

"Aha!" he exclaimed to himself, "these shoes turn out to be my own. I just saved us a big fight and myself from leveling a wrongful accusation!"

A Hankering for Pork Tripe

AN inspector-general who was a student of philosophy developed a hankering for pork tripe that made it necessary for him to partake of a bit every day. But it so happened that due to a prolonged drought, all butchering was ordered stopped as part of the prayer ritual to bring rain, and yet this inspector-general still insisted on having his tripe.

The butchers of the town respectfully submitted that the slaughter of animals was ceased for the duration of the drought, but the inspector-general gave the reply: "Whether or not the slaughter of living beings must cease is not the issue here, I am merely asking for a bit of tripe."

A Belittled Elephant

AN emissary from Annam brought an elephant to China to be given as tribute to the imperial court, drawing the attention of many bystanders along the way. "This elephant is too small!" one of them was heard to comment.

"How can you say it is small?" replied the emissary. "Because I have many elephants at home and they are *all* bigger than this one," answered the bystander.

"The imperial court alone is entitled to the ownership of elephants. If you have elephants on your property, I shall report it to the court," the emissary retorted. The man then got down on his knees, saying: "I have no elephants at home — I was only talking big."

The Fortune-Teller's Son

THE son of a fortune-teller refused to learn his trade. This angered his father, who admonished him. The son replied: "But the trade is really all too simple for me!" The next day, a man came to their home amid a rain storm to seek advice. The father told his son to take over for him in order to test him, so the son promptly asked the man: "Did you come from the northeast?" The answer was affirmative. "Your name is Zhang?" "Yes!" "Are you seeking advice on behalf of your wife?" "Yes!" came the answer again. After the session was over, the man went away convinced.

The astonished father asked his son: "How was it possible for you to guess all those details from the outset?" The son replied: "The wind was blowing from the northeast when he came in. He must have been walking west because his back was soaked. On the handle of the umbrella I could see the characters for 'Qinghe' prefecture carved, and knew the surname of someone who hails from there could not be other than Zhang! In such weather he could only have been sent for a reading on behalf of his wife; certainly not by his parents, or on his own initiative!"

The Plagiarist

SOON after Yang Heng had retired to seclusion on Mount Lu, a candidate plagiarized his writings on an answer to the imperial examination, and was passed. Yang was later granted a degree as well, after he spotted the irregularity. Confronting the plagiarist, Yang demanded: "Did you or did you not employ the line 'The cries of cranes soar to the heavens one after another'?"

"Knowing how highly you valued it," replied the man, "would I have dared take it?"* "For *that* I can pardon you!" responded Yang.

The Boatman's Find

IN the study of elocution, a man picked up the high-sounding phrase *qi you ci li* ("That's preposterous!"). As it struck his fancy, he employed it often. One day in a fit of panic at a river crossing he forgot the phrase and began pacing up and down on the ferry nervously, hoping it would come back to him. The ferryman asked what he had lost, and when he replied that he was searching for a word, the boatman roared: "How can a phrase get lost? Why, that's preposterous!" The man then exclaimed: "Why, you've found it! Why didn't you tell me earlier?"

---

* A rather ordinary line in common parlance among poets, the plagiarist obviously felt no one would have claimed exclusive right to it.

Lined Garments

A poor scholar was still wearing thinly-lined garments deep in winter. Someone asked him: "Why do you yet wear garments with such thin lining in this cold?" "In unlined clothing," he replied, "I would be even colder."

Sharing One Pair of Shoes

TWO brothers pooled their savings to buy one pair of shoes, which they shared. But the elder brother usually put them on as soon as he got up in the morning and continued to wear them all day. This obliged the younger to have to wait until night to get his turn with them. After the elder had gone to bed, he used to get them out, put them on, and then would walk from place to place all night long until they were finally worn out. The elder brother then suggested: "Let us again pool our money and purchase another pair." But the younger replied: "No, thank you, I would prefer to get some sleep!"

The Vanishing Herb

A man was given a sort of grass by someone he had met known as a "vanishing herb". Anyone who held the grass, he was told, became invisible to others. Grass in hand, the man promptly seized some money from someone in the marketplace and ran off with it. But his victim rushed toward him and commenced to give him a thorough trouncing. "You might be able to hit me, but you'll never *find* me!" heckled the thief as he was beaten.

Seeing a Good Joke

A blind man was sitting in a crowd. When the crowd laughed on seeing something funny happen, he laughed too. On being queried as to the reason why he did so, the blind man replied: "Since so many people were laughing, I figured it *must* have been a good one!"

Better to Be Blind

AS they were walking together, two blind men mused: "The blind are truly the most fortunate people in the world. Those with good eyes have to spend their days slaving away, particularly all those peasants! They will never know the splendid luxury of our leisure!" But their words were overheard by some farmers who, pretending to be officials, shouted at them to make way and, because they were unable to do so in time, ordered that they should be beaten with a hoe handle. They were then ordered to make haste in leaving the place. As they did so, however, one of them was overheard to say: "It is still better to be blind. People with sight after they get beaten would be sentenced as well!"

False Incrimination

EACH taking with him an amount of money as capital, two merchants were on their way to another town for business endeavors. Many days away from their home town, one set upon the other and tried to beat him to death in an isolated place. Leaving him for dead, he took his money and returned home, telling the victim's family that the man had perished of a severe illness contracted *en route*. His relatives found no reason to doubt the veracity of this story, and, later, he even married the victim's wife. Unexpectedly, however, the man he had left for dead regained consciousness and eventually found his way home after a long period of recuperation.

A complaint was then filed with the district magistrate to the effect that: "A man was beaten to death by the accused with the object of seizing his money and then his wife."

But the magistrate rebuffed the plaintiff and said *he* should be held for investigation on the charges of slander and false incrimination, arguing: "How can one who is still alive be said to have been beaten to death? Thus, there was no force or duplicity involved in the marriage since he has sent money and presents for the wedding."*

---

* Referring to the capital and estate of the "murdered" man.

from **A Record of Zen Wit,** a Ming collection by Pan Youlong

The House on the Wayside

A traveling scholar decided to try to get a room in a house on the wayside for the night. There he found only a lone woman at the time. "No one is in at present!" she told him, leaning against the door frame. "What about you?" asked the scholar. "I mean there's no man about," she stammered. "What about me?" the scholar replied.

The Benefits of Meditation

A Zen Buddhist monk preached to one of his congregants on the benefits of meditating all night long through to the next morning. Very late one night at the toll of the fifth bell, it suddenly occurred to this congregant that a certain man had on a certain day obtained on loan a load of barley from him which he had never repaid. He woke up his wife to tell her, proclaiming: "Now I have at last discovered the benefits of sitting up all night in meditation that the monk was so keen on. Why, I was almost cheated by that man out of a whole picul of barley!"

Rowing

WHEN Luo Wenxue was sailing to Jingzhou, he ordered his doltish servant, one Ersheng by name, to do the rowing. The servant protested: "But I cannot operate the oar." Luo then spoke harshly to him, but the servant answered: "How can *I* lead when *I* don't know the way?"

Something to Eat with the Wine

A youth fond of sarcasm once rode over to the house of an elderly neighbor to mooch some wine. The old man lamented: "I have wine but nothing to offer you to eat with it." "Butcher my horse, then," said the youth. "But what will you ride?" asked the old man. Pointing at a chicken, the young man said: "I shall ride that." The old man replied with a smile: "I would have offered to kill the chicken for you, but alas, I have no firewood!" "Cook it with my robe, then," replied the youth. "In that case, what would you wear?" asked the elder. The youth pointed to his bamboo fence, saying: "That fence would do nicely."

Books Are Printed

A friend of the family exhorted a youth to devote himself to reading, so the latter stayed inside his study for a number of days.   Eventually he came out to thank the friend for his advice, adding: "Indeed, books are worth reading!   I only thought they were written by hand!   Now I see they are printed."

The Lazy Pauper

A thief broke into the house of an impoverished man. Finding nothing worth stealing, he fled, leaving the door open.   From his bed, however, the pauper screamed out: "Close the door behind you!"

"No wonder you're penniless," exclaimed the thief, "if you're *that* lazy!"   But the pauper replied: "What's the use of striving for anything if it all ends up getting taken by people like *you* in the end?"

from **A Treasure-House of Laughter,** compiled by
Feng Menglong of the Ming

Three Men

THREE men were sleeping alongside one another on
the same bed when one of them felt an itch on his leg.
Half-asleep, he scratched the leg of the man on his right
side. Since that failed to ease the itch, he continued
scratching till the man's leg bled. The second man
reached down and touched the wet spot of blood on his
leg and, thinking that the third was suffering from
enuresis, woke him up immediately. The third complied by getting up and going out to urinate. But next
door there was a distillery, from which a constant dripping of mashed grain and rice could be heard. Listening to this, the third man just kept standing there till
daybreak, thinking that the sound of the dripping was
that of his urine hitting the ground.

Parents for Sale

A foolish son was looking after his father's store when
the old man was out on business. A man appeared and

asked: "Do you have *zunweng* (a honorific term for someone's father) here?" The reply was: "No!" The man again asked: "Is *zuntang* (a polite reference to another's mother) here?" The reply was also "No!"

The father, on learning what had come to pass during his absence, said: "Look, by *zunweng* he meant your father and *zuntang* refers to your mother."

The son seemed vexed and after some time exclaimed: "How was I to know the both of you were for sale?"

How Did the Character Grow?

A father taught his young son to identify the character *yi* — for "one" — written with a single stroke. The next day the son was standing nearby when the father happened to be wiping off a table. Using his rag, the father wrote with one swipe the character on the table's surface but the child failed to identify it. "I taught you this very character yesterday," growled the father. "How then did it grow so much overnight?" asked the astonished boy.

The Account Book

A county official who was illiterate drew pictures on his account book when he wanted something purchased. A superior official who was on a tour of inspection arrived one day when the county official was out. The superior examined his books and indicated disapproval of this way of doing things by striking out the pictures with lines of red ink. On his return, the county official became angry at his underlings and shouted: "So you have bought one box of red candles for use in the office, so what? Why go recording that all over my account book?"

The Official's Birthday

ON the birthday of a district official his subordinates presented him with a golden rat of lifesize proportion because he was born in the year of the rat (one of the twelve cyclic animals symbolic of the year in ancient China). The official was very pleased, but made sure to let the remark drop: "Did any of you know that my wife's birthday is also coming up shortly? She was born in the year of the ox."

Joint Production

TWO men were discussing the joint production of wine. One said to the other: "You shall supply the rice and I the water." The second asked: "If all the rice comes from me, how shall we apportion the finished product?" The first man who had made the proposal to begin with replied: "I shall be absolutely fair about the whole thing. When the wine is finished, each gets back exactly what he put in — I'll siphon off the liquid and you can keep the rest."

The New Skirt

A woman going out in a new silk skirt threw her shoulders back, fearing lest she should fail to attract the attention of others, and pranced down the street with her nose in the air. After some time, she paused to ask a boy: "Are they looking at me?" "No one is out just yet," replied the child. She then relaxed her shoulders and lowered her head a bit, remarking: "Well, at least I can have a *rest*!"

The Master's Belly

ONE day a master told his servant: "While you are out on the town you should talk up everything at home in order to gain face for our family as well as yourself." The servant took this injunction to heart.

On running into someone who was saying that the San Qing Hall was a very magnificent building, he exclaimed: "Why, it is only equivalent to *one* of the many buildings our household has available for rent!"

Another man remarked on the enormous size of a dragon boat. But the servant responded: "Yes, it is roughly the size of one of the canopied boats used by our household for pleasure sailing."

A third man noted an ox that was extraordinarily fat. The servant then added: "His belly is no bigger than that of my master."

Died of Fright

A number of men who were sorely intimidated by their wives called a meeting to discuss ways and means of retaining some semblance of dignity as men. Someone who wanted to put a scare into them walked in and announced: "The wives of you gentlemen have all learned of this gathering and have resolved to come here *en masse* and fight this thing out with you." All those present, except for one, dispersed immediately in great panic.

It was thought that this lone man had mustered the singular courage to stand up to the whole lot of their wives, but upon examination it was found that the man had died right then and there in his seat of sheer fright.

A "Double-Axe Hacking"

A man's sickness was traced to excessive drinking and too much sex. His physician cautioned him to abstain from such practices with the parable that this way of doing things was tantamount to hacking away at something with two axes.

His wife looked askance at the doctor who, understanding her reaction, swiftly changed his line and said: "If you can't abstain from sex you should at least stop your drinking."

The patient replied: "Amorous acts are more deleterious to health than drinking. These should be avoided first!"*

"If you only listen to part of a doctor's advice, how can you expect to be cured?" retorted his wife.

---

* According to traditional Chinese medical theory, the sex act depletes the male of vital fluids, causing a gradual weakening of the *shen*, an organ identified with either the kidneys or testes. Excessive consumption of liquor also effects the *shen* adversely, both being deleterious to the general well-being.

Gritting One's Teeth

THE mother and daughter-in-law in a household were both widows. The former always reminded the latter: "Being a widow requires one to grit one's teeth sometimes in order to make it through life alone."

In a few weeks, however, the mother-in-law began to carry on an illicit affair with a man. When the younger woman voiced objections, reminding her of what she had repeatedly advocated before, the crone opened wide her mouth and chortled: "But you see, I have long since run out of teeth to grit."

Machismo

DURING a beating inflicted by his wife, a hard-pressed husband wiggled underneath the family bed. "Come out this instant!" the wife demanded.

"I am man enough to do as I well please!" he replied. "And I'll come out when I'm good and ready!"

Collapsing Trellises

THE clerk of courts in a certain yamen, who was constantly being intimidated by his wife, was scratched on the face by her one evening. On the morning of the next day, when he went into work at the yamen, the magistrate queried as to the nature of his scars. The henpecked clerk tried to hide the truth, claiming that: "Last night, while strolling in the yard to take in the cool of the night air, a grape trellis collapsed on me and cuts from the wooden beams left these scars today on my face."

His superior, however, was not to be convinced by such an explanation and declared: "Only a wife could be capable of this! Send forth the yamen runners to bring her here this instant!"

Quite unexpectedly, however, the magistrate's own wife had been hiding in the next room and overheard all that had just been said. She was enraged and charged out into the court. Panic-stricken, the magistrate cried out to the clerk: "Court's in recess! Clear the court! My own trellis is about to fall!"

A Portrait of the Deceased

A man who had feared his wife all the time that they were together finally summoned forth the courage to shake his fist at her portrait displayed before her funeral bier as a gesture of his many years of pent-up hostility toward her. At that exact moment, a breeze stirred, causing the paper portrait to turn as if in response. Petrified with fear, the man immediately retracted his hand, stammering: "Ju-, ju-, ju-, just teasing!"

Hospitality

THE hospitality of a certain man had become much touted, even to the extent that some compared him to Lord Meng Chang of old, who permanently lodged, fed, and entertained a retinue of three thousand house guests or "retainers" as they were called. Someone who learned of his magnanimity was so impressed that he betook himself to the portals of this nigh-legendary host.

Upon arrival he noticed a conspicuous silence and a dearth of human activity. Inquiring of a neighbor as to the whereabouts of the throng of guests, however, he was informed that since it was presently the luncheon hour, they had all returned to their respective homes to take the noon-day meal.*

---

* The point of "retainers" is that you feed them. As in most cases of Chinese hospitality, the entertainment of guests largely focuses on the meal.

Borrowing Tea Leaves

A man who had a guest in his home sent someone to borrow a bit of tea from a neighbor. The tea, however, was not forthcoming. As he was waiting, the host kept adding cold water to the pot to keep the water from boiling away. The longer he waited for the tea leaves, the more nervous he got and the more water he added until the cauldron was full. His wife then suggested: "Since this is a close friend, why not invite him for a bath instead of tea?"

Giving Out Dates

A certain man was so stingy he would never invite anyone over for anything. When once he was persuaded to lend his place out to a neighbor to hold a banquet on the premises, someone noticed the preparations under way and asked a servant if the master of the house was planning to host a feast. "You'll have to wait until his next life if you want to see my master doing anything of the kind!" the servant snapped at the passer-by. "What," screamed the master to the servant, "did I hear you say? — Who authorized *you* to give out any dates?"

An Aversion

WHEN a starving scholar came within sight of a market vendor selling *mantou* or steamed buns, he let out a feigned wail and collapsed on the ground nearby. When the puzzled vendor asked him what the trouble was, he replied: "I have this aversion to *mantou*!" Trying to derive some fun out of a most peculiar occurrence, the vendor then placed ten or so of these buns in an empty room with the scholar and shut the door. After a short time had passed, he flung open the door and found most of the pile of buns devoured.

In reply to harsh questioning, the scholar simply stammered: "For some inexplicable reason, I suddenly lost my aversion." Angered by so boldfaced a deception, the vendor retorted: "Pray, have you any other aversions?" "At the moment, sir," came the reply, "I have none, save for an incredible loathing for two cups of good, strong tea."

A Love of Peace and Quiet

A man living between a blacksmith and a coppersmith was annoyed by the continual racket coming from the two establishments, as he was by nature a man who cherished tranquility. In fact, he announced more than once that should they ever choose to remove from their respective premises, he would host a banquet in their honor.

One day, the two smiths came to him and said: "We shall soon be moving and would be glad to accept your former offer of a feast!" Asked for the dates of their removal, they both replied: "Tomorrow."

Overjoyed at the indication of a specific date so close at hand, the man hosted the dinner for them that very evening, after which he asked: "Pray, where will each of you gentlemen be relocating?"

"I shall remove to *his* shop, and *he* to *mine*," answered both of the smiths in unison.

Locating a Noted Doctor

THE King of the Nether World dispatched an underling to pay a call on a noted doctor in the world of the living with the instructions that the doctor could be found at a place free from haunting by the vengeful spirits of those whose deaths had resulted from malpractice.

But everywhere he went the underling met with rancorous ghosts clamoring at the gates of doctors' homes. Finally, he came upon a house which only one lone ghost haunted and said to himself that this must be the house of the noted doctor. On inquiry, however, he learned that the doctor there had gone into practice on the premises only the previous day.

Learn First Things First

A doctor was detained by relatives of a patient who had died of a fatally inaccurate prescription given at his direction. The doctor broke loose and escaped by night, having to swim a long way across a river before he could make it home. Entering his house, he discovered his son engrossed in the study of medical texts, and observed to the young man: "You shouldn't be in such a hurry to master medicine! Learn first things first and start with swimming."

A Prayer to Be Kicked

ON his way back from gathering wood, a woodcutter weighed down by his load stumbled into a doctor on a narrow path. In anger, the doctor shook his fist at the man as if to strike him. The woodcutter promptly knelt down and pleaded: "Please kick me instead!"

Answering a dismayed bystander, the woodman then explained: "Treatment at his *hands* would be far more deadly than his *feet*!"

On the Road to the Afterlife

A doctor who had already caused the death of a sick infant promised the family he would be responsible for delivering the corpse to the house of an undertaker for burial. Fearful of a deception, the family sent a servant along to accompany him. While crossing a bridge on the way, the servant saw the doctor suddenly let a dead infant drop out of his sleeve and into the water.

"How could you do a thing like this to the family?" screamed the servant. — "Now, now!" shot back the doctor. "I haven't done anything to your master's family. *Their* baby is still right here in my other sleeve."

A "Carpenter"?

A craftsman was called in by a property owner to install a bar for locking a door, but he mistakenly nailed the bar to the outside of the door. The owner of the house then reviled his stupidity, calling him a "blind fool".

"You're the one who's blind!" the craftsman retorted. "What do you mean?" the house owner demanded, rather miffed. "If you had any vision at all," replied the craftsman, "you wouldn't have hired *me* in the first place."

Breakfasting on Bran

A local idler came out of his house one day after swallowing some husks to tide him over till his next meal. Fortunately, he soon espied a rather well-to-do acquaintance, an official of some rank, who invited him aboard his boat for a meal. The idler, for form's sake, insisted that he had already partaken of a large quantity of dog meat* at breakfast, so that only a single drop of wine would do. After drinking to excess, however, he got sick and vomited, whereupon the host exclaimed: "You told me you breakfasted on dog meat; what's this chaff I see here?"

Embarrassed, the idler looked askance for a bit, but then muttered: "It *was* dog meat. The finest dog is that fed exclusively on grains!"**

Drink the Wine Cold

A man who was fond of **drinking once had** a dream in which he had obtained **a rice wine of rarest** bouquet.

---

* Thought to be a delicacy by some.
** The flesh of dogs fed only on grain was considered the highest of several grades.

As he was about to heat it up before drinking,* he suddenly awakened from his dream. Sorely regretful, he exclaimed: "Would that I had only drunk it cold!"

Li San Lao

A man was about to enter a certain city, carrying with him a long bamboo pole higher than the lintel of the city gate. Cutting the pole to a length permitting passage through the city gate did not seem at all a practical solution, and the bearer of the pole became extremely perplexed as to what to do until advised by a passer-by to consult a certain Li San Lao, reputed to be a man of great wisdom, who lived three or so miles away. At this juncture, Li happened to appear riding on a donkey toward the city. His presence was favorably received by a large crowd of admiring townspeople, who surged forward to greet him. But on noticing him to be riding on the hind end of the donkey, someone asked the reason why he did not choose to sit squarely on its back. Li San Lao replied: "The reins are much too long!"

---

* Rice wine is normally warmed before being served.

Wine Tasting

A penurious father-son duo agreed to budget their wine expenditures to one cash only per day. In view of the fact that so limited a quantity of wine could easily be exhausted, they further agreed to check the speed at which it could be consumed by drinking it only from the tips of their chopsticks, which they dipped into a small quantity of wine. But one day when the son was seen to be dipping twice in succession, his father sullenly rebuked him, saying: "Let's not gulp our wine, son!"

Dread of Water

A man with a dread of water had never set foot on a boat in his life. One day when traveling, he had to cross a river, so he instructed his companions to tie him to the boat with the rope extra tightly. On reaching the other bank, as they were about to remove the rope, he realized that on his return journey he would have to cross the same river again. So he said: "If a second crossing is unavoidable, I would prefer that we simply pay the ferrymen to move the boat ashore, lest it not be tied as securely for our second crossing."

A Fifty-Fifty Ratio

A man known for his most greedy and avaricious disposition was once told by a rich person: "I shall present you with one thousand silver coins if you will agree to allow me to flog you to death." After a long pause, the man replied: "How about beating me half to death. In that case you pay only five hundred."

Disguised

GOING out for occasional business, a debtor took to wearing a round-bottomed basket on his head in the hope that his creditors would not be able to identify him. But one day in the street he was recognized by one of them. Tapping on the basket over the man's head with his fingernail, the creditor asked him: "How about the agreement we have reached?" "Tomorrow!" came the answer from underneath.

Very soon a heavy downpour began, and raindrops started tapping on the basket disguise in rapid succession. The man, whose vision had become impaired by a combination of the rain and his own sense of panic at the tapping, began to cry and shout: "I'll pay you all back! Everything tomorrow!"

On Avoiding a Second Fall

A man chanced to fall down a second time, just after he had gotten up from an earlier tumble. At that point he observed: "Had I known a second fall was in store, I should not have arisen the first time!"

A Token of Thanks

IN tears, a girl about to be married off asked her sister-in-law: "Who formulated the institution of weddings and marriage in the first place?" "The Duke of Zhou,"* answered her sister-in-law, whereupon his name was subject to great abuse by the bride-to-be. But on her first visit home after the first month of being married, she queried: "Whatever became of that Duke of Zhou?" "Why do you ask?" replied the sister-in-law. "I'd like to darn a pair of slippers for him as a token of thanks," replied she.

---

* A figure credited by the Confucians with the establishment of a number of rites.

Mounting the Sedan Chair

A certain girl, about to leave home to be wedded, was wailing at the prospect of mounting the sedan chair for the journey to her husband's house. At that moment it became apparent to all involved in the ceremony that the bearers could not find their carrier poles. "Oh heavens!" stammered the bride between sobs, "they are over there by the corner of the gate!"

To the Bridegroom's House

A bride was weeping uncontrollably in her sedan chair on the way to the home of the bridegroom. Unable to bear such agonized sounds of grief, at length one of the sedan chair carriers said: "My lady, we are at your service and shall carry you back to the home of your parents, if that be your desire."

"I'll stop, I'll stop!" she shouted as the sobbing ceased.

Habit

WHEN slicing meat at home a cook concealed a piece under his jacket. Noticing this, his wife rebuked him, saying: "That meat belongs to us; why are you hiding it?" The cook responded: "I forgot!"

Needing a Thousand Hands

AN apprentice barber had to press with his finger any point of the scalp injured through the slip of his razor, so as to stop the bleeding. Since he was not yet well practiced at the art, he came one day to the conclusion that: "A barber's is no easy job, fit only for Guanyin (the Goddess of Mercy), since she boasts a thousand hands!"

from **The Expanded "Treasure-House of Laughter"**, also comp. by Feng Menglong

A Subtle Gesture Is Inimitable

A man ordered his son: "Follow your tutor in his every word and act." One day when the son was dining at his tutor's house, he tried to imitate his mentor in every act of eating, drinking and bodily carriage. The tutor noticed what was going on and had to keep himself from laughing out loud at the boy. Finally he laid his chopsticks down and sneezed. Unable to follow suit, the youngster excused himself, saying: "Such subtlety is beyond me!"

The Oath of Officialdom

A civil servant convicted of accepting bribes was fortunate enough to fall under a general amnesty. When set free he swore an oath to refrain from taking bribes in the future, saying that if he so much as touched his hand to graft in any form, boils should grow upon it.

Not long thereafter, a man offered to pay him off in order to receive a favorable judgment in a suit. Because of his vow, however, the official was reluctant to accept the money with his hand. After a pause to consider the situation, he suggested to the other party: "Since you have already shown yourself to be so considerate, would you mind terribly slipping it into my boot?"

Latrine Keeper

A petty official was grossly avaricious and coveted anything of value that came his way. He was shamelessly greedy for bribery and had done something to almost every member of the public in his locale, when one of his cohorts remarked facetiously to him: "Judging from your activities, the only administration in which *you* could not extort bribery would be that of a public latrine."

"Well," he replied, "if I were placed in charge of a latrine, I should deny entrance to wealthy persons who had to go, then they would need to bribe me to get in! Conversely, in the case of those who avoided the stench and did not want to come near, I should drag them over and act as though I would throw them in. Would a bribe not then be forthcoming?"

The Correct Way of Marching

A contingent of new recruits arrived at their barracks where the officer in charge attempted various ways and means of extortion. At the first drill session, he ordered the soldiers to march forward, which they did, but the officer promptly dressed them down, saying: "Now I have to follow you."

Complying with a second command, the men about-faced and marched in the reverse direction. But their commandant once more reviled them, saying: "You cowards are putting me out front!" The recruits were at a loss as to what to do after such initial failures, so they knelt down and begged of him the correct way of following orders.

"Present me with a monthly sum," replied the officer, "and you may march any way you like."

Conveying an Urgent Document

IT was urgent that an important document be delivered as quickly as possible. The official responsible had provided an underling with a swift mount for this purpose. The lackey then proceeded to drive the horse before him at a gallop. Seeing this, someone politely suggested: "Why not *ride* the horse on so urgent a mission?" "Six legs should prove quicker than four," replied the messenger.

The Venerable Prankster

LAOZI, the founder of Taoism, once proclaimed: "If the holy scriptures are recited a thousand times, the supplicant shall rise above the purple clouds." There was one Taoist practitioner who believed in the literal truth of this instruction. After chanting the scriptures 999 times, he went through the ritual ablution, mounted a terrace, bade good-bye to his friends and relatives, and prepared to levitate into the clouds. He then recited the scriptures for the thousandth time, but, though he remained standing there until dusk, not a wisp of cloud appeared, to say nothing of the levitation taking place. The Taoist then turned to his statue of Laozi and sighed: "Even a man of your venerable age is capable of a hoax!"

"Insects Are a Delicacy"

ON his return from a venture, a merchant told of all the wondrous things he had seen by rivers and lakes.* "After passing through the Yellow Ox Gorge, the mosquitos there were as big as ducks, and after crossing the Iron Ox River, the mosquitos were of the size of a goose." His wife interjected: "Why didn't you bring

---

* i.e. on the road.

some back to eat, then? Insects are supposed to be a delicacy." "To eat?" replied the man. "I'm just lucky *they* didn't decide to eat *me*!"

Fish from a Well

A man was host to a tutor, providing him with board and lodging. At every meal they dined on fish, but only the fish heads and tails. Finally the tutor ventured to inquire from whence the fish came. "They are raised just outside in my pond," replied his host. "Your 'pond' must be a well," ventured the tutor, "otherwise they would not be so short."

Destined for Each Other

A man, who was quite a miser, was also known for being easily pleased or readily vexed. One day he bought a small piece of meat and asked his wife to prepare some soup with it. The meat, however, sunk to the bottom of the bowl when served, where it became invisible through the grease on top. The man then got outraged at his wife and reviled her, saying: "We must have been enemies in some former life, because everything you do in this one is designed specifically to irk me! Let's just separate and do it right away!"

But a moment later, after his chopsticks chanced to hit on the meat at the bottom of the bowl, he was bursting into laughter, slapping her on the back and making jovial remarks like: "We must have been destined to meet for five hundred years!"

Sour Wine

WHEN a customer at a tavern intimated that their wine had gone sour, the outraged tavernmaster promptly had him strung from the rafters. Answering the query of a passer-by, the owner proclaimed: "My humble tavern stocks only the finest of wines, but this fellow has impugned them as vinegar; should he not hang for this slander?" The passer-by then asked to sample a cup, whereupon he knitted his brows and said to the owner: "Set that man free, and let *me* hang in his place!"

A Wealthy Village Ox

DURING the Spring and Autumn period,* a unicorn**

---

* 770-476 BC.
** In old China the unicorn was considered the most auspicious of all mythical creatures. Its appearance could preserve a dynasty, one of the things Confucius sought to do.

appeared in the western part of the state of Lu, but the rustics there did not know it to be an animal of divine omen and killed it.

Confucius himself went to see it and had to wipe the tears from his eyes with the sleeve of his raiment. Fearing lest their master die of grief, his disciples covered an ox with copper coins, in an attempt to disguise it as a unicorn. They then beckoned to their master to look, crying out: "The unicorn! He lives!" But after the sage had dried his eyes and looked again, he sighed: "What could be auspicious about a village ox with money?"

"And Don't Take Credit!"

A simple rustic, who had become wealthy by means of extreme parsimony, was unable to die despite a protracted illness. On his sickbed he told his wife one day: "I have acquired sufficient wealth for us only by living a frugal life and severing links with all clan and relatives. After my death, I want you to follow in my footsteps. Start by skinning my body and selling the skin to a leather craftsman's shop, the flesh to butchers, and the bones to a lacquer factory."

Only after pressing his wife to assure him she would heed this as his last will did he give up the ghost. After half a day's interval, however, he regained consciousness to admonish his wife, saying: "In this day and age people are totally unreliable; therefore, I came back to remind you not to accept credit!"

Those With Money

A gardener failed to keep eggplants alive, which vexed him enough to make him seek the advice of an old and experienced planter. The latter told him to bury a copper coin beside each eggplant. Asked why this would work, the old hand replied: "Have you not heard the saying: 'Those with money can survive anything'?"

"For a Penny More...."

A man who was by nature extremely parsimonious came upon a flooded stream. Reluctant to pay the ferry fare, he began to wade across the rising waters. By the time he got to mid-stream, however, he was knocked over by the swift current which began to carry him down-river for some distance.

His son, who was on the bank still, sought help to save him. A nearby boatman demanded a coin of a certain denomination, but the son only offered half the amount, whereupon bargaining proceeded for quite a while. Coming up for the last time, the father shouted in the direction of his boy: "Son, don't go a cent over half! If he still wants a penny more, forget it!"

A Violent Temper

THERE was once a man who was all too easily irritated. One day he noticed someone still wearing a thick felt hat on a hot day in July. Deeming the wearing of such a hat inappropriate to the season, he attempted to strike the man for this breach of fashion. After some time he was persuaded to go home by a crowd that had formed, but he soon fell ill as a result of this fit of temper, recovering only after some days.

After the twelfth lunar month, at the time of the Spring Festival,* his younger brother took him out for a stroll one day. On spotting a man wearing a felt hat approaching from a distance, however, the younger brother bolted ahead toward him and said: "My elder brother has just recuperated from an illness. Pray, would you kindly keep clear of him for a while?"

Determination

A father and son were both quite obstinate. One day the father had invited a guest over for drinks and dinner, so he sent his son into the city to purchase some

---

* Usually in January or February, when the wearing of such hats would be deemed appropriate due to the cold weather.

meat. On the way home with the portion of meat, the son noticed someone walking straight toward him. They both started through a narrow gate at the same time, and neither was willing to make way for the other, standing, instead, face to face with one another for the longest time.

Trying to find out what had happened, the father eventually located his son at the city gate, where he promptly told him: "Take the meat home and keep our guest company at dinner. I shall stand here for you and face this bloke down."

A Parvenu

A parvenu whined of his discomfort upon re-entering the house after having ventured out to look at the flowers in his garden by the early morning sunlight. When his wife asked what ailed him, he replied: "When I was examining the flowers I was spewed upon by dew that dropped from a rosebush I had bumped. Do call in a doctor to effect some cure!" The wife replied: "You have already forgotten your bitter experiences when we first met as beggars. We were drenched that night in a nightlong downpour in a bamboo grove. How is this any worse?"

Laundry Time

A certain scholar had only one cloth raiment to his name. As he had nothing to wear when it was being washed, he was forced to stay in bed the whole day long, until it had dried. A visitor came calling one day and asked his son where the father was. "In bed," replied the son. "He must be sick, then, what ails him?" queried the visitor. "Is it sick to go to bed when you have nothing to wear?" replied the son.

Affectations

A poor man was invited to a great feast at the home of wealthy relatives. Having no fur coat to wear, he donned a thin garment made of grass material and went on his way thither. Fearing lest others should ridicule him for such scanty attire, he wielded a fan and told all the guests at the feast: "I have, by nature, an aversion to hot weather and have taken to using a fan even in the dead of winter."

By the end of the party, the host had become painfully aware of this ploy. He then decided to play along with it, arranging for a bed to be prepared for him with extra-thin sheets, grass pillows and, of course, no blankets in a pavilion outside by their pond. Unable to withstand the cold, the poor relative got up in the middle of the night and prepared to abscond with the bedclothes wrapped around him, but tripped over the sheets and landed in the pond.

The host stood on the side of the pond, looking at him in dismay and asked what had happened. "'Tis this aversion of mine to the heat," replied the poor relative, "though I was provided with a bed in a pavilion, I still needed to have a dip in your esteemed icy pond before retiring."

Climbing the Stairway to Heaven

WHILE attending dinners with their father-in-law, the sons-in-law of a certain family often forced the least fortunate of their number to take the most obscure seat in the house. Feeling this to be a loss of face, the man's wife advised him to rush into the seat of honor, but the young man didn't quite appreciate the idea.

One day when he was going together with his wife to the home of his father-in-law and the guests were asked to take their seats, the wife gave him a signal to rush to the head of the table. Her husband saw that there was a differentiation in height and, noticing a ladder in the dining hall, pressed up against an eave, he ran straight to it and climbed up half way.

The wife gave him an angry glance, but failing to fathom the reason for her vexation, he yelled back: "How high do you want me to climb, to heaven?"

Planning a Livelihood

ONCE there was a man extremely fond of hearing praise from the mouths of others. A physiognomist, noticing this aspect of his character, spoke highly of him in his presence and added: "Your bright eyes are indicative of a wondrous fortune throughout your life."

The man was very taken with this remark and feted the physiognomist for days, even lavishing expensive gifts upon him. On parting, however, the physiognomist told him: "There is one thing you ought to keep in mind." "That is...?" he asked. "You really need to find a vocation! A pair of eyes is hardly enough to see anyone through!" replied the physiognomist.

from **General Chatter, Past and Present,** comp.
by Feng Menglong

"We're All One"

ONCE when a scholar was explicating the thesis that all things of nature are one and the same entity, a pedant challenged him, saying: "By that do you mean that a man enlightened in the Way can subdue dragons and cow tigers before him? I suppose you are saying that if one such man met a fierce tiger he could ride upon its back at will and would run no risk whatsoever of being devoured by the beast simply because 'we are all one'?"

Zhou Haimen, who was present at the time, laughed at their exchange and commented: "Riding on a tiger's back indicates that a division between two bodies still exists, but once the man has been swallowed into the tiger's belly, they are indeed one." At this, the bystanders chuckled.

How Chen Gao Limited His Drinking

CHEN Gao of Nanjing loved wine, and so when he was assigned a post in charge of education in Shandong, his father was apprehensive that he might do something wrong and lose his job through over-indulgence. He thus wrote his son, warning him to avoid excess.

As a result, Chen Gao, always the filial son, spent his first salary to commission an artisan to make a golden goblet for himself with the huge capacity of two catties, bearing the inscription: "Remember thy father's words: Only three cups at any sitting." This quickly became a watchword among the literati of the area.

The Joys of Inspiration

ZHU Yehang, a scholar of Fengmen and tutor at the house of a man named Wang, had a penchant for writing poetry. One evening after he had dined with Wang, as the master of the house returned to his own quarters at the end of the supper, the old tutor, gazing at the full moon overhead, was inspired to compose these lines: "Nothing is better than the cup in hand. For in a year, how many times can we notice the moon o'er head?" Because he was pleased with this couplet, he knocked so forcefully on the partition, beckoning the master to rise out of bed to hear it, that everyone in the house thought fire or theft must surely be the reason for such clamor at night. When the master found out what the cause actually was, he simply plopped back down at the dinner table, shaken, and said, "Well, let us have a drink then...."

Pushing

IN the olden days a man from the state of Yue enjoyed great fame as an accomplished swimmer. One day his wife was seen floating an infant on the water at the age of only one year. Answering someone who was astonished at so early an attempt at coaching, she boasted: "Well, his father is a good swimmer so the baby should be too."

"X Marks the Spot!"

WHILE crossing a river, the sword of a man from Chu fell from the boat he was riding on into the water. He hastened to place a mark on the side of the boat, telling his companions: "This is exactly where the sword fell." When at last the boat came to shore, he stepped out and waded through the shallow water there, groping around for his sword just below the mark he had made on the side of the boat.

Do Two Errors Negate?

A profligate son always did things in defiance of his father's will. On his deathbed, the father told him: "You must be sure I am buried in some body of water," thinking that since the son inevitably acted contrary to anything he ever said, the body would, of course, be entombed on dry land as a result.

But the profligate said to himself: "Throughout his entire lifetime I have always disobeyed my father. But now that he is dying I must not fail him again!" So he promptly had a pond dredged on their property for the express purpose, and threw his father in.

Wishful Thinking

A girl in the state of Qi was the object of courtship by two neighboring youths. One, the eastern neighbor's son, was ugly but quite rich. The son of the family to the west, on the other hand, was handsome but poor. Failing to come to a conclusion as regards the choice, the parents left the matter up to their daughter to decide. The girl favored an acceptance of the courtship of both neighbors, justifying this solution to her mother by saying: "Would that I could board on the east, but lodge to the west!"

A High Official's Duties

THE greedy and corrupt Zheng Renkai was once a district official of Mizhou. Once when his servant pointed out to him that his shoes were worn out, he called in a subordinate official who was known to always be wearing a pair of new ones and gave him the order to climb up a tree to pick fruit. The servant then stole the shoes the subordinate official had left on the ground at the behest of his master. The subordinate protested this to his corrupt superior, who would only reply: "A district official is not supposed to spend his time guarding the shoes of others!"

The Delicious Dish That Came Too Late

MU Ning was a prefectural governor in the Tang dynasty; his son, a secretary of a minister, was responsible for his father's food. Whenever the governor was in the least displeased, he ordered a flogging. One day, when the son was on duty to supply food he hit upon a number of new and different recipes. Delicious dishes of bear meat and venison were served up for the governor as a result. Mu Ning partook of these to his fill. All around envied the likely recipient of the reward they thought surely in the offing.

On a full stomach, however, the governor ordered a flogging all the same on the grounds that "such delicious dishes had never been supplied earlier".

Let Us Test the Whip!

DURING the Sui dynasty, Yan Rong was appointed governor of Youzhou Prefecture. During a tour of inspection he came upon a thicket of bushes that he thought would make particularly good whips, so he had one taken down in order to try it out on someone.

The man selected for the test pleaded that he had done nothing wrong, but Yan Rong insisted: "If you commit a crime in the future you are herewith exempted from flogging." The man did eventually commit a petty offense and was about to be scourged for it when he reminded the governor: "You promised me exemption from flogging." Yan Rong replied: "Yes, that applied when you were innocent. But what about now that you are guilty?"

The flogging then proceeded.

Bridegroom Needed

IN the Tang dynasty noble families often chose to marry their daughters off to those young scholars who passed the examination. Most of the scholars who were chosen did so against their own will. A smart-looking youth who would have been the envy of any aristocratic family was taken by some nobleman's servants to escort back to his mansion. The youth appeared happy enough to comply, and was not the least bit shy. On arrival at the mansion, a man in rich attire came out eventually and announced to him: "Our young mistress, a girl of great beauty and integrity, is agreed to marry you." The young man then made a deep bow and said: "I am indeed elevated by this honor. I must, however, first return home to consult with my wife." At that, crowd assembled outside the portals of the mansion dispersed amid great laughter.

Half a Day's Respite

ONCE when a man of high position was visiting a Buddhist temple, after having imbibed a sufficient quantity of wine, he recited a poem written in Tang times: "Passing by a bamboo grove I chanced to converse with a monk. Yet another occasion for half a day's respite in this floating life."

On hearing this, the monk who was hosting him laughed, and when asked of the reason for his laughter, replied: "Your Excellency has indeed had half a day's respite, but I have been busy for three days in preparation for your arrival."

from **The Best of Decorous Humor,** a Ming compilation by Zui Yue Zi

The Lost Hoe

A farmer returned from the fields one day and his wife asked him where his hoe was. The husband replied in a loud voice: "I left it in the field!" "Don't speak so loudly," cautioned the wife, "lest our conversation be overheard and the hoe stolen as a result." She then urged him to go back and get the hoe but when he did return to the field in search of it, he failed to find it. He then went back home again and on seeing his wife, bent down and whispered gingerly into her ear: "It's gone!"

A Naked Official

A low-ranking official, sweating profusely after a long day of sundry affairs, entered a public bath house to cleanse himself. After the bath he discovered that his robe and underwear had been stolen. The manager of the bath house, however, grew suspicious that the man was attempting to perpetrate a hoax. The official then donned his cotton cap, pulled on his boots and fastened his sash to his otherwise naked waist and asked the manager: "Could I have walked in dressed like this?"

The Talisman

A man bought an amulet to ward off mosquitos, fastening it to his body, but it yielded no results. He then went back to complain to the seller, who advised him, in turn, that it had not been applied in the proper place. Answering his question as to which was the proper place, the seller replied: "Underneath a mosquito net."

Excessive Salt

TWO young brothers were filling their bowls with steamed rice when one asked what dish they were going to get to eat with it. Their father replied: "That salted fish being smoked over there on the kitchen stove. Take a mouthful of rice first and then have a look at the fish." Not a moment later, the younger of the two suddenly cried out: "Number-one brother looked twice!" "Too much salt will kill him!" replied the father.

An Old Calendar as a Present

ON New Year's Eve someone sent a New Year's gift to a man who promptly took down his old calendar and handed it as a tip to the messenger. But the man's domestic servant reminded him that an old calendar would probably be useless to the man. "Well," replied his master, "'tis of no great use to me, either."

Theft?

A man was put in a cangue* for stealing an ox. Although well aware of what he had done, when an acquaintance of his asked him: "What has happened to you?" The man replied: "It was just rotten luck, that's all. While walking leisurely on the street I noticed a straw rope and picked it up thinking that it might come in handy at some future date." His acquaintance responded: "Surely no one could be convicted for so simple an act!" "But," the man continued, "there happened to be a small calf tied to the end of the rope."

---

* A large wooden collar similar to the stocks, but borne by the prisoner instead of being fastened to the ground.

A Hempen Quilt

ONCE when a man complained of the number of mosquitos he encountered in the summer, a friend told him: "Then it would be best for you to sleep beneath a lined hempen quilt at night." Asked for the reason, the friend replied: "When the mosquitos try to bite, the shaking of the outer cloth will be so rough as bend their stingers, a vital organ for mosquitos. That will require some 120 days for them to recover. By the time they are ready to make fresh attacks on you, cold weather will have already set in."

"Venerable Sir"

WHEN bandits entered, the occupants of a house tried to appease the leader by addressing him as "Your Majesty", "Commander", and finally "Liberator", yet he seemed pleased at none of these. Finally they made discreet inquiries as to how he wished to be addressed and he replied: "You may address me as 'Venerable Sir'." When asked why he preferred this to the other titles he replied: "Because our civil officials are all addressed in that manner."*

---

* Implying that they (the civil officials) are the greatest bandits of all.

A "Water Chestnut Tree"

A mountain villager went to a lakeside district. Resting beneath a tree, he found a water chestnut on the ground, which he ate and found most agreeable in taste. Standing up, he tried shaking the tree violently, both at the base and branches, but nothing fell down. "Such a large tree with only one nut!" he mused.*

Evading a Debt

A debtor not only refused to make good on his word, but further deceived his creditor, saying: "At present I am courting a rich widow. The only thing is that I do not have enough money for a betrothal gift. If you could find it in your heart to help me out, I shall have enough money not only to repay you but to lend to you in the future!"

Believing his words, the creditor extended him further loans. Once he had the money, the debtor used a portion of it to repair and redecorate his house, causing the creditor to think it a more plausible story.

One day the creditor was passing before his gate and decided to knock at the door. Inside, he heard a

---

* Water chestnuts (*lingjiao*) grow in the water as part of an aquatic plant, not as nuts on trees.

woman's voice call toward the door: "My husband is out presently." This same response was repeated on several other occasions. Growing suspicious, the creditor finally peeped through a hole in one of the paper windows. There he saw no woman at all in the room, only the debtor standing there himself impersonating a woman's voice and pinching his nose with his fingers.

The enraged creditor broke in through the window and a flurry of blows descended upon the man, who just stood there taking it, with his nose still pinched and yelling: "If my husband owes you, what has that to do with me!"

Impetuosity

ON his approach to a noodle stand, there was a man who had already begun screaming: "Why haven't I gotten my noodles yet?" The vendor took a bowl of noodles, poured them on the table, and shouted back: "Go on, eat, hurry up! I need to have the bowls and dishes back right away to be washed out." The man went home in a huff and revealed the incident to his wife, saying: "I almost keeled over from anger! How offensive can one get?" On hearing that, his wife hurriedly packed her bags and told him: "Well, if you are going to drop dead, I am ready to re-marry."

After spending only one night with the second husband, he sent her away. She asked what had transpired and he replied: "I expected you to give birth to a son right then and there."

Search Me!

A man whose ox had been stolen filed a complaint with the district administrative office. The officer asked the plaintiff: "When was it taken?" — "Tomorrow," replied the man. At that the officer unwittingly cracked a smile. The district official saw this and shouted at the legal officer: "*You* stole it, didn't you? Where have you concealed it?" But the officer merely shook his sleeves and said: "Search me!"

Red Trousers

ON an inspection tour, an official noticed a frivolous young blade sauntering down the street. The wind was blowing that day, and a gust revealed him to be wearing red satin trousers beneath an outer robe. The official ordered that he be subjected to ten strokes of the bastinado for the extravagant affront. After the fifth stroke had fallen, he stood up and protested, saying: "Five are enough! The upper half of my attire was of ordinary hempen* cloth!"

---

* Indicative of sobriety and frugality.

from **Present-Day Humor,** a late Ming compilation

A Desire for Food

A child was crying and told his father: "I'm hungry!" The father walked over, patted him and said: "My son, just tell me what you want to eat. No matter if it be dragon's liver or phoenix marrow, I shall obtain it." "But I just want ordinary food, nothing else," replied the child. "Brat!" shouted the father. "You always ask for something we don't have!"

The Hardest Substance on Earth

TWO persons were involved in a discussion about what the hardest thing on earth was. One claimed it was iron, but the other replied: "No, iron can be smelted with flame, so it can't be the hardest thing." "What then is the hardest?" replied the second. "It has to be the human beard," answered the first, "for no matter how thick the facial skin,* it can still work its way through!"

---

* In Chinese someone described as having "thick facial skin" is someone without a sense of shame (i.e., his face is so thick nothing can penetrate or affect the insides, hence he does whatever he pleases without regard for others).

from **Hua Yan Qu Le Tan Xiao Jiu Ling,** a Ming compilation

Just Plain Quilts!

A quilt maker cut costs by using straw as his quilt. But his idiot son revealed this to someone. The father then instructed: "If ever thou art asked, just call them quilts and no more!"

One day the father got up early to go out with a friend. Seeing a straw dangling from his beard, the son exclaimed: "Father, father, there's a quilt in your beard!"

A Liar Gets His Comeuppance

TWO families were united by marriage. The father of the groom, who was rich, invited the father of the bride to his house, where he had all his family's valuable heirlooms on display. He then asked his poorer in-law: "Have *you* anything like *this*?" The father of the girl replied: "Yours are merely lifeless things, for which I have little admiration. But as to my house, we keep there two living treasures." "What are they?" demanded the groom's father. "A divine crane and a giant sea horse," replied the father of the bride. "Let me have a look at them, if it be your pleasure," replied the groom's father.

The father of the bride gave him a date on which to come and then bade farewell. Returning home, he became deathly worried for he could think of no way to show the treasures he had spoken of to his in-law on the appointed hour, so he told his son in answer to his query: "I uttered a lie yesterday to my son-in-law's father, and I can think of no plan to put him off any further. You see, I told him that we have a divine crane and a sea horse at home to make him think we were important." "Worry not, father," replied the son. "I think the situation salvageable. Set thy heart at ease, await the appointed date and I shall take care of everything."

When the father of the groom did come, the son of the other had dressed his own father in the robes and regalia of an immortal and sat him upon a great throne in the center of their hall. "Where is thine illustrious father?" demanded their rich in-law. "My father was forced to leave on some unexpected business," replied the youth. "But he told me to come to have a look at a sea horse and a crane," said the in-law. "Oh!" replied the young man, "unfortunately neither are here at the moment, either. Our great sea horse was borrowed by the dragon king for a ride on the ocean, while the crane has been taken off by a fairy for a flight to attend the Divine Feast of Peaches in honor of the Queen Mother of the West."

The in-law then pointed to the young man's father seated in the middle of the hall in all his regalia, asking: "And what manner of divinity have we here before us?" — "That," replied the lad, "is our relative, His Majesty the Wizard of Lies!"

Weak in the Sphere of Human Affairs

BEFORE a visit to her parents' house, a young bride coached her simple and incompetent husband, saying: "My parents have two famous paintings mounted on scrolls. These are family heirlooms and known widely by the titles: *Han Gan's Horse at the Side of a Stream in the Wilderness* and *Dai Song's Ox by the Shore of Green Willow Dyke*. If you are ever shown these two paintings," she continued, "be prepared to identify them by title."

While at the home of his father-in-law, the latter did show him the paintings and he repeated exactly what he had been taught to say by his wife. The old man was pleased that he could identify the paintings.

Later, the old man brought out a scroll depicting eighteen famous scholars and asked the son-in-law what he thought of it. But the young man merely repeated the titles he had uttered when the first two scrolls were shown him earlier.

As those present broke into a fit of laughter, finally the father-in-law sneered: "You know your oxen and horses, but when it comes to people, forget it!"

Do Good Deeds While You Yet Have Time

ONCE, long ago, there was a Buddhist monk who exhorted others to make donations to the temples, to give alms to monks and to worship the Buddha, so that in the other world they would not be subject to the horror of being cut in two with a saw by the King of Hell.

Not long thereafter, it came to pass that both this monk and a chief patron of his temple died. The monk was promptly placed upon the chopping block in Hell because of the grievous nature of his worldly sins. On seeing what was about to transpire, his chief patron ran over to ask how such a thing could have happened to the monk. But the monk himself explained: "You don't understand! The King of Hell knows that in the mortal world the temples are being abandoned and that holy men have become fewer and fewer. Hence he desires that each monk be sawed in two in order to double the number we still have left."

A Henpecked Magistrate

ONCE there was a district magistrate who was known to live in dire fear of his wife. While in court one day he heard the sound of quarreling in the outer compound and ordered his attendant to find out what was wrong. The attendant returned and reported: "There is a fight going on between a couple in the guard room and the woman is beating the man." The magistrate clenched his teeth as he listened in anger and shouted: "Why, if I were in his place, I'd. . . ." Just at that moment his wife poked her head out from behind a screen and yelled: "You'd what?" "If I were in his place," replied the frightened magistrate, "I would kneel down and take my beating like a man!"

from **Rolling in Laughter,** compiled by Chen Gaomo
during the Qing dynasty

Precious Cargo

A father and son were carrying a large keg filled with
wine, but one faulty step caused the keg to fall and
break. Immediately the son got down on the ground and
began drinking as fast as possible. After a while he
looked up at his father and said: "What are *you* waiting
for — someone to bring some dishes to go with it?"

Non-Identification

A certain glutton always ate non-stop every time he
was invited to attend a dinner party. One day he paused
to remark to one of the other guests at the dinner table
that they had met at a similar occasion once before.
But the other guest answered: "No, I think not ...
perhaps you have mistaken me for someone else."

When more dishes were brought out, the man lowered his head and began to exhibit his voraciousness,
wielding his chopsticks first in this direction, then in
that, without halt. On seeing this, the other guest remarked: "Why yes, we did meet once before. The only

thing was that you never looked up from the dishes, so I never caught a glimpse of your august face. Forgive the oversight!"

Sneak Eating Ahead of Guests

THERE was a host who, while his guests were sitting in the courtyard, always used to sneak back inside the house to have first crack at the food. One day, however, one of the guests observed in a loud voice: "This is such a magnificent dining room, too bad all the beams and pillars are being eaten by termites!" "What?" snapped the host as he came running. "Where are they?" "Well, you can't see them *now*," replied his guest. "After all, all the eating *here* is done inside!"

Eluding Bandits

A rather naive man, on hearing the entry of a thief into his courtyard, hurriedly pasted up a notice outside the inner-chambers reading: "No Admittance!" When the thief had broken into the ante-chambers, he quickly pasted another reading: "No Exit," and withdrew to the inner-chambers. When those had been violated, he fled to the toilet. The thief, however, was onto him by that time and approached the toilet stealthily, whereupon the master of the house pressed his hand to the door and, coughing, called out: "Toilet's occupied!"

The Eighth Indispensable Item

A certain wife was fond of drinking, but her husband kept refusing to supply her with wine, pointing out: "They say there are seven items indispensable to a married household, and those are: 'Fuel, rice, cooking oil, salt, soya, vinegar and tea.' But I don't see wine on that list!"

The wife retorted: "Wine is required before the household begins to function; it should *at least* have been bought the previous night, so why should it be included in the seven items?"

The Burn

AN old man fell asleep after drinking too much wine one winter's night. He had a coal foot-heater in the bed and slept with his leg too close to it, burning his foot. In the morning he complained bitterly to his family members who were living with him, saying: "I drank too much last night and, of course, I could not feel that

my foot was burnt! But what about you all? Why
didn't you do something, all you youngsters? Do you
mean to tell me you didn't smell anything?"

Evil Thoughts

A monk who was traveling in the same boat as a woman
of some status kept ogling her. The woman grew angry
at his impertinence and ordered that he be beaten. The
monk then shut his eyes. But upon arrival at their des-
tination, the woman had him beaten once more. "What
have I done now?" the monk exclaimed. "You were
thinking about me with your eyes closed," she replied,
"and that's even worse!"

Euthanasia

A young scholar who was learning to practice medicine
never paid close attention to the required readings about
various medicines and their side effects. After taking
the pulse of a patient, he would dash off just any
prescription and tell the patient to get hold of it and
take it. A number of his patients died as a result, one
after another. Finally their relatives began to complain,
saying that he should own up to his responsibilities. To
their charges he replied: "What? You didn't know?
That was a mercy killing!"

Something to Sit On

THERE once were two brothers, the elder one rich and the younger one poor. The younger one asked: "Why are you rich, brother?" — "Because I offer up pigs and sheep as sacrifices to the tutelary god," replied the elder. The younger brother then told this to his wife, who remarked: "We can easily do that as well. Here we have two stools. They, too, have eight legs. Why not offer them up in lieu of a pig and a sheep?"

The husband did as she said, but the tutelary god was enraged. The man's wife then tried to placate him, saying: "Although there is nothing to eat, at least you can offer your guest a seat!"

from **The New and Expanded "Collected Jokes",**
compiled by Zhao Tianyang of the Qing

Wearing Out One's Welcome

AFTER their drinking bout had finished, two men lingered on in a wine shop for hours. Finally the distraught shopkeeper looked up at the sky and commented: "Looks like it is going to rain soon!" But the two customers then exclaimed to one another: "Well, if it's going to rain now we certainly can't go anywhere. Let's wait until it's over!" Much later the owner walked over to them and said: "I think the rain has passed." At that point the one turned to the other and said: "Why bother leaving now that there's no storm to worry about!"

from **A Good Laugh,** by Shi Chengjin of the Qing

A Centenarian's Worries

A centenarian was known for his longevity, wealth, and large household. On his one-hundredth birthday, numerous guests filed into his gate to offer congratulations. Knitting his brows, the old man took on a look of consternation. Those present reminded him: "You should be in the midst of celebration now, what worry is it that darkens your countenance?" He replied: "I have nothing to worry about, save that by the time I reach my two-hundredth birthday, the number of guests coming to offer congratulations will have increased by a hundredfold or more, so how shall I keep them all straight?"

A Reluctant Tailor

A tailor was called in to cut material for a suit. Sizing up the material for some time, the tailor was still reluctant to apply his scissors and begin cutting. In reply to the customer's query, he answered only: "If the material is cut to fit you, nothing will be left for me, and if I pocket a yard or so, the garment will certainly be too small for you.* So how can this job be salvaged?"

Abstinence

A monk was a guest at a private dinner. Remembering him to be a holy man, the host asked if he should be served wine. The monk replied with a smile: "I have been known to drink a bit, but I abstain from all that vegetarian fare."

Filial Devotion

A doctor was called in to treat a patient, but he diagnosed the condition as hopeless, adding that the only possible remedy would be if a filial son would make bold enough to hack a piece of flesh off his own thigh as a curative dietary supplement.

The patient's son replied at once that the flesh would be forthcoming.

After the doctor's departure, the son went out with a knife and, it being summertime, soon found a man sound asleep outside the gate. He thereupon cut a slice of flesh from the man's thigh.

---

* Referring to the practice of tailors keeping part of the material as a "tip", whether with the customer's knowledge or otherwise.

The man arose in a fright, screaming with pain. But the youngster merely waved a hand and cautioned him not to carry on, saying: "Your flesh is going to save a dying father. Don't you understand the importance of filial piety?"

Way to Get Rid of Pains

A man who had a malignant tumor on his leg was in extreme pain. He then bored a hole in the wall through which he stuck the afflicted leg. Asked for the reason, the man replied with knitted eyebrows: "Because I can no longer bear the pain of the tumor, I have no choice but to dangle my leg outside of my house, in the hope that the pains may pass out of it and into another."*

The Comeuppances of Malpractice

A quack physician had two children, a son and a daughter. But he eventually had to forfeit his son to

---

* Part of the humor here has to do with the identification between the self and the home. Because the pain has "left" the home of the sufferer, it is as good as out of his body.

another in compensation for the death of an infant under his care. His daughter suffered the same fate due to another fatality brought about by his negligence. Then he was left with only his wife in a state of loneliness and despair.

A man one day chanced to knock at the door, seeking medical consultation. "Who is the patient?" the doctor called out. "My wife," replied the comer.

The doctor, on the brink of tears, announced to his wife: "Woe is me! Someone has taken a fancy to you."

Inhibition

A drinker was in the habit of acting silly no matter how much wine he had, which was, in turn, greatly resented by his wife. One day at home, he asked for wine and his wife gave him water that had just been used to ret the fibers from flax. In no time he was acting as silly as ever, carrying on and being boisterous. His wife then reviled him, saying: "Cursed of heaven! That was only ramie water I gave you. How do you expect anyone to believe it got you drunk?" But presently he broke into loud guffaws and announced: "I *thought* there was something wrong. That's why I still felt so inhibited!"

An Astute Observation

A rich old man was plagued with constipation and could eliminate only after expending great effort. Finally, an observer made the suggestion that he should hire someone to move his bowels *for* him.

"Pray, Let the Blade Strike Higher"

AT the execution ground, a convict told the headsman: "Since I am to die, then let it be done, but pray let the blade strike me high upon the neck!" When the executioner inquired as to the reason for this unusual request, his victim replied: "I have a boil on my lower neck, and, were the blade to strike the boil, that could only serve to intensify the agony!"

The Moon in the Capital Is Rounder

ON his return from a visit to the Northern Capital, a fellow continually went on about how great the place

had been. One evening when he was walking together
with his father in the moonlight, a passer-by remarked:
"What a fine moon!" But the braggart who had just
returned from the capital lost no time replying: "The
moon in the imperial city is much finer than this."

At that, his father shot back angrily: "Nonsense!
There is only one moon in the heavens that shines over
the earth, so how could the moon in the capital possibly
be any better?" He then slapped his son's face. The son
then sobbed: "Quite a blow, but the fists in the capital
hit harder!"

A Man Who Speaks Highly of
His Son

A father and son were walking down the street together
one day when someone who had never seen the boy
paused to ask who the youngster was. The father replied: "He is the son-in-law of a direct-line grandson of
the ninth generation of the minister of the Civil Office,
favorite of the imperial court, and he also happens to be
my own son!"

Working Off a Debt in the Next Life

A rich man summoned several debtors to his house and said: "If you paupers are truly penniless, you should just swear an oath to me that the debts you owe me will be repaid in the next life. After that I will consign your I.O.U.s to the flames."

Overjoyed, the man who had borrowed the least amount from this wealthy patron said: "It is my greatest desire to be reincarnated as a horse in the coming life, so that I may serve as your loyal mount, master, and work off my debts that way!" The rich man then nodded and burned his I.O.U.s forthwith.

A second man who owed him a little more made the vow that "after reincarnation I shall come back as an ox to labor at your every project as a means of repayment!" This pledge was also accepted and his I.O.U.s were sent to the flames, too.

The last of the debtors who owed much more than the other two exclaimed: "In the next life I wish to come back as your father as a means of repayment." "What?" shouted the rich man. "You owe me debts of this much silver, which you have consistently failed to make good on, and then come back with this insult! What an outrage!" The rich man was about to hit him, but the pauper began to explain: "Listen, I owe you so much already that the debt can never be repaid with the labors a horse or an ox perform. But as your father, I could live frugally, accumulate fields, real estate, and a huge fortune for you by working until the end of my days and never stopping to enjoy any of it myself. Would that not be the best way of satisfying the debt?"

A Good-Sounding Epitaph

A woman Wang by name, who was very wealthy, wished to have a flattering inscription carved upon her coffin. To this purpose she paid a large sum of money to a Taoist. After much thought about what to write and how to phrase it, the Taoist could not think of anything really appropriate that would make her sound important; finally he decided that the best he could legitimately do was: "Here lies Mme Wang, formerly next-door neighbor to a noted lecturer of the Imperial Academy and Ceremonial Provost of the Imperial College."

Make Concessions to the Rat and Bee

A rat and a bee became sworn brothers, inviting a licentiate to join their alliance. The scholar had no choice but to comply, and was ranked third in the hierarchy. Someone who learned of this weird pact asked: "Why are you, a scholar, ranked below a rat and a bee?" "Because," the licentiate explained, "of the two, one is a master at squeezing through small openings and the other at stinging people,* so I have to make concessions to them."

The Dumb Speak!

FEIGNING dumbness, a beggar often pointed at his alms bowl as a mute gesture towards potential benefactors, while he gasped at them. One day he strode into a wine shop with two coins for a drink. As the tavern-master finished filling his bowl, he said: "Add a bit more to it!"

"You could never talk when you were in here before," exclaimed the astonished barkeeper, "how is it that you speak now?" "Before," answered the beggar, "I did not have the money, so what could I say? Now I have two coins, so everything is different!"

"It's Even Stronger over Here!"

A rich old man was entertaining guests when suddenly he broke wind. "Ah!" exclaimed one of the guests

---

* Here, "squeezing through openings" and "stinging" imply shameless opportunism and careerism perpetrated at the expense of others.

seated near him. "Though that sounded like a fart, it did not stink in the least!"

"Not only did it not stink," blurted another, "it bore a distinctly appealing scent!"

"What?" exclaimed the rich man, with knitted brows and a worried countenance. "Why, I've heard it said that if a person has gas, but no strong smell to it, his inner organs have begun to malfunction and death draws nigh. Is it true? Have I long to live?"

Suddenly the first guest began fanning the air in front of his face ferociously with his hand and insisted: "The smell *just* wafted over this way!"

Not to be outdone, the second wrenched up his nose, contorting his face, and finally pinched his nostrils tightly shut with his thumb and forefinger, exclaiming: "It's even stronger over here!"

The Words Will Not Ring True

A man went to a Taoist temple and asked that his fortune be told. "First," said the priest, "you must donate incense money, otherwise the divination might not be as accurate as possible. Without such a donation, in fact, none of it will come true!"

The Rotting Tray

THERE was once an official who, at the time of assignment to a higher post, swore to the gods: "If I should accept bribe money with my left hand, let it rot before my very eyes; and if with the right, let it suffer a similar fate!"

Soon thereafter, someone offered him a bribe of much gold, but out of fear for the consequences of the oath he had sworn, he said to himself: "I shall simply extend a tray upon which the metal can be placed and tell the interested party to drop it in. When I swore the oath I said 'money', not gold. In addition, I shall not touch it with my hands. That way, if anything is to rot it should be the tray, which will have no connection with me!"

Let Me Be Your Baby!

AN aged man, who was very wealthy but emaciated and feeble, always hated it if someone reminded him of his poor physical condition. But if they were to pay him some insincere, exaggerated compliment implying good health and sturdy stature, he would light up with joy. With this in mind, a man decided to exploit the situation and gain favor with him as a prospective patron, telling him: "Though your hair has turned white, your skin is still tender and young looking, comparable not only to that of a child's but, in fact, just like that of my new-born babe's!" The old man was elated, and responded: "Why, if my skin were just a touch more delicate, I should surely wish to *be* your baby!"

Birthday Wishes

WHEN an old man was accepting congratulations on the occasion of his one-hundredth birthday, one of the well-wishers exclaimed: "May our illustrious old friend live to be 120!" At this, however, the old man became frightfully angry, saying: "What is this? I'm not eating off your family's money. Why limit my years so drastically? Why should you not wish me 200 or more?"

Exaggeration

WHEN two men met, both displayed signs of irritation on their faces. The first queried: "Why does your face show such indignation?" The other replied: "I live in the Middle Kingdom, yet no sound escapes my ears, no matter if it comes from thousands of *li* away. While sitting in meditation of late, I heard a monk chanting in the Western Paradise. The noise of his chanting disturbed my inner peace, but he ignored my pleas to desist. I became enraged, picked up Mount Sumeru, and hurled it at him like a little stone. Quite unexpectedly, the monk, on seeing the mountain plummeting toward him, merely rubbed his eyes with his hand and said: 'Whence comes this dust to impair my vision?' Thereafter, he went on with his infernal chanting. My might failed to sway him in the least."

Then he inquired of the other man: "What is it that vexes you?" The second replied: "Yesterday I had a guest in my home, but was caught with nothing to offer him. So I captured a mosquito, took out its heart and liver, cut these into 120 pieces and then fried them for a dish to serve him. Who could have predicted that the guest got a piece of the liver stuck in his throat! Then he complained that the slices were too big! Moreover, he is still staying with me at present and just keeps complaining."

The first man then responded: "How could anyone have such a narrow throat?"

"Since you have ears with an auditory range reaching all the way to the Western Paradise, and since there is someone whose eyes hardly even blink when confronted by the vastness of Mount Sumeru, why can't there be a throat narrow enough to gag on a piece of mosquito entrails?" responded the second.

Uniforms Are Provided

WHILE being entertained in the sitting-room of his host, a guest saw a servant enter, bringing tea, but devoid of all clothing, save for two tiles which were hanging from a belt around his waist to cover his lower extremities. "When a guest is here," said the master gruffly, "why are you wearing such awkward clothing? Go change to something lighter!" The servant complied with the order, and soon returned sporting two lotus leaves in place of the tiles. The guest then remarked to his host: "Life in your mansion is far too immodest, much to the detriment of the frugal management of household, I fear." The master replied: "No, it is hardly immodest!" The guest responded: "Take your servant, for instance. He has both a thick outfit and also a sheer one, to say nothing of the other arrangements you must have made with him for the housekeeping. Think of the expense!" "When I first interviewed him to engage his services," replied the host, "he promised that he would go home to his *own* house for all meals and that I would only be responsible for providing uniforms. So, you see, the quandary is that if I don't provide him with at least *two* alternate outfits, it would be difficult for me to maintain the terms of the contract!"

Beggars and Dogs

SOMEONE asked a beggar: "Why do dogs always want to bite you as soon as they see you?" "Because," responded the beggar, "a dog can only judge a man by his clothing."

Smoke as Excrement

A rich old man refrained from engaging servants, taking care of all his domestic affairs alone, but only at the cost of much effort. A number of his friends tried to persuade him to engage a servant for this purpose, but he would always say: "Of course, I know the benefits of having a servant, but the only trouble is that I should have to pay and feed him. That is why I choose to rely on my own labor and refrain from engaging anyone."

In order to challenge him, a friend finally said: "In my house I have a manservant who requires neither pay nor food, yet he works diligently. I am willing to lend him to you to work for free. Will you accept or not?" The old man paused to query: "If he takes no food won't he starve to death?" "This servant," replied the man, "met an immortal when he was young who taught him the secrets of inhaling wind for food and passing smoke as excrement. Hence, he *never* feels hungry."

On hearing this, the old man paused and at length

shook his head, saying: "No, thank you, I don't want such a servant." "Why?" asked the friend. "Well, you see," replied the old man, "I really would like to get his share of nightsoil for the fields, you know, and if the person of whom you speak passes only smoke, well, then I'm afraid I can't really use him around here. . . ."

Retractility

ONE day a father lectured his son, saying: "Retractility is an important element in rhetorical style; cut and dry statements, on the other hand, are a pitfall," but the son interrupted and asked: "What do you mean by 'retractility'?"

At this juncture, a neighbor came in with a request to borrow some household articles from them. The father told his son: "Now see here, if someone wants to borrow some items, you should say neither that you have everything nor that you have nothing. Merely reply that some are available to lend and some not. This is the essence of retractility in speech. It applies to many other human affairs as well." The son made sure to take his father's words to heart.

On another day, when a visitor came and inquired: "Is your honorable father in?" The son replied: "To a certain extent, yes; to a certain extent, no. . . ."

The Elixir of Immortality

A doctor about to die called out while lying on his deathbed: "If a skilled doctor can be located to cure me, I shall offer him a dose of my secret elixir of immortality as a token of gratitude. Tell him my elixir will enable him to live for centuries!"

Someone in attendance then asked: "If you possess such a remarkable medicine, why not take it yourself?"

"A good doctor," he replied, "doesn't go around writing prescriptions for *himself*!"

A Scholar's Verdict

A villager once foolishly revealed his desire to be rich, boasting: "I shall be satisfied only when I possess one hundred *mu* of land." But his resentful neighbor replied: "If you ever got one hundred *mu* of paddy fields, I would be the first to raise ten thousand ducks to devour all your rice!" The two began to quarrel unceasingly and eventually decided to file suit against each other before the magistrate.

Not knowing the location of the magistrate's yamen, they eventually found their way into the gate of a red-walled college of Confucian scholars. One scholar happened to appear before them in the hall and they took him to be the magistrate, each presenting his case before him. The scholar then said: "*You* go on with *your* plan to buy the fields, and *you* to raise the ducks. When *I* take office *I* shall be ready to pass judgment on the case!"*

"Don't Ruin the Pelt!"

A man was seized between the jaws of a tiger and being dragged off when his son, in an attempt to save the father's life, dashed forward with a knife and made ready to stab the beast. At that moment the man shouted from within the tiger's jaws: "Son! If you have to do any chopping, I want you to start with the paws. There's no sense in ruining a good pelt!"

The Emperor and His Imperial Robe

BACK from the Northern Capital, a beggar boasted of having seen the emperor. Answering a question as to the attire of the emperor, he stated: "His Celestial Majesty wore a crown of the finest carved white jade and a robe forged of gold." Then someone asked him:

---

* Referring to the fact that most scholars never took office due to their failure to pass through the exacting examination system.

"But how could one perform any rites of obeisance when attired in this robe of gold?" The beggar scoffed at this query and replied: "You really know nothing of the ways of the world! Does the *emperor* have to bow to anybody?"

The Proper Positions of Religious Heads

IN the main hall of a temple a statue of Laozi was situated at the left and one of the Buddha on the right. Noticing their positions, a Buddhist monk said: "Our Lord Buddha's creed is the more widespread, so why should he be relegated to the right of Laozi?"* He then reversed the statues, moving Buddha to the left. Soon, however, a Taoist priest noticed this discrepancy and was aghast, exclaiming: "Taoism has always been the most sacred creed in our land — why should Laozi stand to the right side of the Buddha?" He then restored the figures to their original positions.

There followed thereafter a rash of switching back and forth until the two clay sculptures began to crumble. Laozi then turned to the Buddha with a smile and said: "We were both originally doing fine in our respective positions, but those devotees of ours have certainly proved our ruination."

---

* In ancient China the position of honor was the left.

A "Rough" Moon

WHEN speaking with others, a man was accustomed to employ modest appellations for everything his own. One day he had a guest over for some drinks and, as the moon appeared, the guest exclaimed with great enthusiasm: "What a beautiful moon we have this evening!" The host quickly clasped his hands together and replied, in utmost modesty: "Nonsense! You flatter me too much! At my humble abode, even the moon is unseemly!"

"Idiot!"

TWO brothers went to visit a friend. As they took their seats at a table on which dried flat peaches had been laid out, the younger brother, who was totally ignorant, asked: "What is this?" The elder one replied: "Idiot!" Thereafter, olives were served as the second appetizer. The younger brother again asked: "What are these?" and the elder gave the same reply. At the end of the visit, while on their way out of their friend's gate, the younger brother was heard to announce to the elder: "You know, the first idiots had a pungent bite, but at least they were sweet; however, the second batch of idiots was just too gamy for my taste."

Sawing Wine Cups

RESPONDING to an invitation for a drink, a man found that each time the host offered him wine he filled only half the cup. At length the guest asked him: "Have you a saw here? I should like to borrow it for a moment." Asked for the reason why, he replied: "Well, since the upper half of the cup is not being used, I thought it only practical to saw it off. After all, it serves no purpose!"

A Pain

AT a tea party the host was astonished to see one guest wolf down almost half the walnuts in a large dish at one fell swoop. "Why are you just eating walnuts?" he asked in puzzlement. "Because," replied the guest, "they are good for the lungs." With knitted eyebrows, the host added: "Yes, you are undoubtedly benefiting your lungs through dietary supplement, but what of *my* pains?"*

---

*i.e., the pains taken by the host have been set awry by one inconsiderate person. There is a word play at work here also.

Humpback

A doctor boasted of his skills in treating hunched backs, claiming that "any hunchback, be he bent like a bow or a prawn or even if his head be twisted to the waist, can be rendered as straight as a pen by my treatment".

One hunchback, believing his advertising, asked for treatment. Before the operation commenced, the surgeon obtained two wooden planks. One was put on the ground and the patient told to lie on it. The other plank was then placed on top of him, and the patient sandwiched between the two. The ends of the planks were then linked with ropes and the doctor began to slowly tighten them, pulling the planks together. The patient soon began to scream for the operation to stop, but the doctor ignored him completely, increasing the pressure. Finally the man's back was pressed straight, but the patient was killed in the process.

The spectators were outraged and began beating the doctor, who protested: "I was only contracted to right his hunchback; no one ever said I had to preserve the patient's life while I did it!"

Removing an Arrow Stem

IN total agony, a soldier was carried behind the lines after having been struck by an arrow. A surgeon who was called in to treat him assured everyone repeatedly that he could perform the operation. He then took out a pair of scissors and cut off the portion of the arrow's shaft that remained outside the body, demanded his remuneration, and tried to leave. But the wounded soldier himself called out, saying: "Anyone can sever the arrow's shaft outside the wound, leaving the arrowhead still stuck inside. It's the internal wound that I need you to deal with. What are you leaving for now?"

The surgeon shook his head and said: "But I am only a specialist in external medicine. What I can do I have done already. Now it is up to you to find a specialist in internal medicine to do the rest!"

An Offering

A Buddhist monk once decided to offer his blood to sustain other living beings and allowed it to be sucked by mosquitos. But by eventide the mosquitos grew too numerous and he could no longer bear the itching. He then began slapping himself everywhere with his hands at random. A puzzled bystander asked: "Since you have made a vow to donate your blood to them, how can you turn on them and start swatting?" "Because," said the monk, "some of them started to come back for seconds!"

A Street Musician

A man was going to play a lute in the street, and many people gathered around to listen, thinking it to be a performance on a fiddle or guitar. But when the musician began to play, the crowd thought the music too insipid and they all soon dispersed, with the exception of one lone man who remained standing there. At length the musician exclaimed: "There is yet one who can appreciate truly fine music! So my performance has not been in vain." But the man replied: "Had I not lent you that table to use as a stand for your instrument, I would have been long gone as well!"

A Thief's Coat Was Stolen

A thief stole into a room where a couple were asleep. Because they were poor and their house bare, the only thing he could espy worth taking was a jar filled with rice which sat directly in front of their bed. The thief decided to steal the rice and take it home to cook, but could find nothing around to wrap it up in. He then removed his coat and placed it on the floor, preparing to empty the jar onto the coat, wrap it up, and make off with it.

Of those in bed, however, the husband was the first to be awakened. Spotting the thief turn beneath the moonlight as he prepared to take the rice, the husband reached out with his hand and got hold of the coat on the floor, stealthily pulling it over toward him until he could conceal it under the bed on which he slept. Jar in hand, the thief turned back around to begin pouring out the grain, but could not locate the coat anywhere.

Suddenly the wife was awakened, too, and began drawing her husband's attention to the strange noises in the room indicating the presence of an intruder. But the husband hushed her nonchalantly, adding: "I've been awake for a long time already and there's no thief here."

"What?" blurted the thief. "*My* jacket's been *stolen* and *you're* saying there's no thief about!"

Salted Eggs

TWO men were partaking of salted eggs one day when one of them remarked to the other: "I often got the impression that eggs have a very bland flavor, with nothing to recommend their taste, but these are good and salty!" The other replied: "Fortunately you happened to be with me when you discovered this delicacy. I can explain the whole process to you, since I know all about it; you see, they get these eggs from salty ducks. . . ."

Malpractice

A doctor was called to the home of a patient for a diagnosis. The doctor assured them it was no serious illness, but despite a long period of confinement and bed rest, not to mention the outlay of enormous sums for treatment, the patient failed to recover. Full of resentment toward the doctor, the patient's family finally sent a servant to his office to register a stern protest.

In a short time, the servant returned home. Asked whether or not he had spoken as harshly to the doctor as they had bade him do, the man replied: "No! I couldn't get a word in edgewise!" "Why?" demanded the family members. "Because," replied the servant, "there were so many other people there voicing complaints and screaming grievances that I couldn't even break through the crowd!"

from **Idle Jottings from Mountain View Pavilion** by
Huang Tubi of the Qing

Cold Springs

BACK from Mount Lingyin,* a man announced to his
wife: "My heart has become cold." "What do you
mean?" asked the wife. "I mean," replied her husband,
"I have just washed my chest at the Pavilion of the
Cold Springs, so if my heart has not been made cold,
then the springs have certainly failed to live up to their
name!"

---

* Near the West Lake in Hangzhou.

from **Lots of Laughs**, compiled by Du Yi Wo Tui Shi
(Hermit from an Isolated Enclave) of the late Qing

A Dreamer's Tryst

THERE was once a youngster of the surname Qi, licentious and unschooled. Early one day he arose and called to a maidservant in his house, demanding: "Did you dream of me last night?" "No," she replied, without further ado.

Thereupon he flew into a rage and shouted: "Now I saw you in *my* dream, and that's for sure, so how can you deny you took part?" Then he flew into his mother's chambers, telling her: "Your impudent maid deserves a thrashing, mother! Last night I met her in a dream, but today she has the nerve to deny it!"

A Poor Memory

A man was appointed to be magistrate of a certain county. On his assumption of office, he issued a warrant for the arrest of a barber outside the north gate of the city. The barber, who was sentenced to 40 blows of the bamboo, had no idea what crime he had committed and inquired as to the charges, while performing the kowtow. The magistrate responded: "I was treated without due respect by you on such-and-such a date in your shop." "But Your Excellency has never been to my humble shop," the barber replied.

The magistrate suddenly thought back on the event and said: "It is so, I never went there." He then ordered the payment of a thousand cash in compensation to the barber and sent him on his way.

It is true that the magistrate had, before his assumption of office, been slighted by this barber from outside the north gate of the city, but the incident had occurred in another county.

from **Record of Jovial Talk,** compiled by Xiao Shi Dao Ren (The Taoist Little Stone), ca 1884 (late Qing)

A Poor Calligrapher

A man was poor at calligraphy, yet he took great delight in trying to write inscriptions for people. One day when a man was passing by him, fanning himself with a white foldable fan, the would-be calligraphy master was unable to resist the temptation, and stopped him, offering to write something on the fan. The passer-by then got down on his knees to him. At that, the calligraphy buff felt awkward and said: "You need not feel so obliged! After all, all I'm *really* going to do is just write a few characters!" The owner of the fan then responded: "Good sir, I know that; with all due respect, I am merely asking that you *don't* write on it!"

The Temptations of Drink

A tutor who was fond of drinking once hired a servant boy who had a taste for wines, and lost much of his stock as a result. For this reason, the tutor hesitated to engage another, telling himself that if he did hire someone, it must be a boy who knew nothing of drink.

One day a friend recommended a boy to him. The tutor showed the boy a yellowish rice wine and asked him to identify it. "A vintage Shaoxing," replied the lad. At that the tutor was displeased, thinking, "Since this boy knows the formal name for the drink, he must also be familiar with its taste." He then refused to take on the lad as a servant. Another boy was then recommended to him by someone else. This time, he showed the boy another wine and the youth replied: "*Huadiao,* sir." "He knows even the finest brands. Certainly he must be a drinker himself," thought the tutor to himself. And this boy, too, was in turn refused.

Eventually, a third boy was recommended to him. This time, however, the boy failed to differentiate yellow and white wines. The tutor was then pleased, entertaining no doubt that the boy was completely ignorant of drink. In turn, the boy was duly accepted for employment.

One day the tutor went out, leaving his studio in the boy's charge and told him: "I have a ham hanging on the wall of the smokehouse and a fatted chicken in the courtyard. Watch them for me. There are two bottles in the inner chamber, one filled with white arsenic and the other red. Don't even touch them! Should anyone be foolhardy enough to drink their contents, his stomach and intestines would burst immediately and he would die within the hour." The tutor repeated these exhortations thrice before departing.

While the tutor was away, however, the boy killed the chicken and cooked it, and then he ate the ham too. Afterwards he swilled down the contents of the two bottles to wash down the feast and was besotted with drink.

Returning home, the tutor discovered the boy sleeping on the floor like a log. Smelling wine, he found the picked-over carcass of a chicken. At that he became enraged and kicked the boy awake.

In tears, the child whined: "As soon as you left I took charge of things. I had everything under control until suddenly a cat snuck in and seized the ham, running off with it. Then a dog came and chased the chicken away to a neighboring courtyard. I was so upset by this spree of misfortunes that I decided to end my life. Remembering your warning about how arsenic is fatal, I drained the contents of the red bottle first, but was still alive, so I drank the white one, too. Now I am reduced to the pathetic state in which you find me, teetering between life and death!"

A Bird Aficionado

IN the north of China, the lark is prized as the *bai-ling niao*, or "the bird that can imitate the singing of a hundred others". One proud owner there went so far as to engage a boy expressly to look after and feed his lark. He frequently brought the bird into the streets for a stroll and displayed it to all in its cage.

One hot day, the bird was to be bathed. Its master told the boy: "Be careful, lest you cause the loss of a feather! For you will pay for it with one of your legs!" After this warning, the man went out on some business.

Now it so happened that the mistress needed the boy to do a task for her, but he replied: "I cannot leave the bird even for a moment. If one feather should fall off I shall lose my leg."

The master was known to fear his wife, and on hearing the boy's words, the lady promptly pulled the lark out of its cage and plucked off all its feathers.

On his return home, the master discovered the molted bird, was beside himself with anger, and demanded: "Who has plucked my prized lark in this manner?" The boy was silent, daring not utter a word.

But the mistress chimed in: "It was I, I plucked it bare! What of it?" The master's voice then immediately took on a lighter note, and he observed: "Well, the plucking really was quite a thorough job, and I'm sure it makes the bird feel cooler than the bath I had ordered for it. . . ."

A Monkey in a Man's Attire

A new official dispatched the bailiff to bring back an individual described as "appearing human yet no human being". This description proved a veritable conundrum to the poor bailiff, who had to go home to consult with his wife. The wife promptly declared: "There is nothing difficult about carrying out that order. Just put a man's hat and clothing on a monkey and escort it to the yamen, and tell them you have brought back someone fitting the description they gave

you! Then your assignment must be considered fulfill-
ed!"

The bailiff acted according to his wife's advice, ob-
taining a monkey, which he dressed up and led off to
the yamen. The official was delighted, offering fruit
to the monkey, which was fairly tame. Treating it as
a pet, he then ordered someone to bring it to the dinner
table for a drink. But unexpectedly, after only one drink
the monkey reverted to bestial behavior, pulling off its
hat and garment and jumping up and down, creating
a great uproar with its screaming.

The official commented: "You animal, know you no
etiquette? Before drinking you appeared human, but
after a drink you no longer even *look* human!"

A Mean-Spirited Bureaucrat
from the Capital

A bureaucrat from the capital, who was very stingy,
was sent to a certain ministry to perform some function
or another. Before entering the ministry, however, he
had his attendant stop and order a bowl of millet flour
soup, drinking it down in front of the attendant, who
was also hungry and wished for a bowl of the same.
The attendant then decided he must ask for the money
to buy himself a bowl in the presence of the other gentlemen, lest the official should refuse to pay for it. The
official paid out twelve cash, but very reluctantly.

After the completion of his transaction at the ministry, the bureaucrat mounted a carriage for home, to be driven by his attendant. The attendant had planned to guide the horse from in front of the carriage, but as soon as they took off, the official began to curse: "Impudent lout! You are not my elder; how can you think to ride in front of me?" The attendant then had to rein in his horse and ride alongside the carriage. But soon the official abused him again, saying: "You are not of the same rank as I! How dare you ride abreast of me?" The attendant withdrew and was left with no choice but to follow the carriage from the rear. Yet the official continued to browbeat him all along the way, complaining about how the dust caused by the horse was intolerable, getting all over everything, etc.

The attendant then alighted from his horse and begged of his master the correct way for him to ride in escort.

"It matters little to me," replied the bureaucrat, "whether you ride or in what position, *so long as you return the twelve cash* I had to spend on your soup *right* this instant!"

Nobody's Fool

A man of phlegmatic temperament bought a pair of boots one day and a short-tempered man happened to ask in passing: "How much silver did you have to pay for the boots?" The easy-going first man slowly lifted up a foot and, displaying his boot, said: "Two and a quarter taels." No sooner had he gotten out the words than the second man seized him, and began to pummel him, screaming: "You slavish imbecile! You paid a total of four and a half taels for shoes! Idiot. . . ."

But the first man kept cool, replying: "If you have objections, you are welcome to air them. But please do so in a calm, collected manner. Now it just so happens," he continued, holding up the other foot, "that this boot was also part of the deal."

Money Demanded by Ghosts

A traveler who had packed up all his belongings was on his way home and passed through Shandong. It happened to be a year of great famine, and a countless number of people had already starved to death. Because of the prolonged disaster, most inns had closed down, and the traveler had to put up at a temple. There, he noticed several dozen coffins in the eastern wing of rooms, but only one in the western wing.

Deep at night in the third watch, hands ghastly and emaciated began to protrude from each of the coffins. One also reached out from the single coffin in the western wing, but that one looked somewhat plump. Surveying the situation, the traveler made bold to put on a smile and greet them, saying: "Piteous ghosts that you are, from a mere glance at your emaciated hands, I can judge what deprivations you must surely have suffered. Are you asking for money now to lessen your sufferings in the other world?" He then placed a coin in each of the hands. Those in the eastern wing retracted immediately back inside their coffins, but the hand from that lone coffin in the western wing remained in the same position as before. The traveler observed: "Well, if one coin does not satisfy you, then I shall have to give you more." Yet after he had loaded it up with over a hundred coins, the hand still remained there. At that point the traveler became angry and said: "You are asking for much too much! Veritably insatiable!" Only when he took out two more entire strings of cash and hung them on the hand did it retract inside.

The traveler was baffled. Being curious, he got hold of a lamp and held it over each of the coffins, reading on those in the eastern wing inscriptions saying who the bodies inside were, that they had been the victims of a famine, etc. But when he came to the coffin in the western wing he read: "Here lie the earthly remains of His Honor So-and-So, District Police Captain of Such-and-Such County."

A Drunkard's Oath

THERE was once a man who could not bear to leave his cup of wine for a single moment during the day. He lived his life in a drunken stupor, until his friends finally urged him to swear off drink for the sake of his health. The man replied: "I did plan to give it up entirely, but the only trouble is that my son is gone away; I am lonely and spend my days pining for his return, and so am forced to drown my sorrows in wine. But I shall definitely cease my drinking when he comes back."

A friend then told him: "We shall be convinced only if you swear an oath." And so the drunkard solemnly swore: "If I do not stop drinking upon the return of my son, may I be crushed by a runaway wine vat or have my throat blocked by a wine cup that chokes me to death or may I fall into a great pool of fermenting wine, there to drown in ignominy!"

After the oath-swearing, the friend queried as to the present whereabouts of the son. "He is somewhere outside the Village of Apricot Blossoms,* where he is currently negotiating a wine purchase on my behalf," came the reply.

---

* A well-known wine producing center in Shanxi. If the son had been sent there, it is probable that he intended to acquire considerable stocks and highly unlikely that the father could resist them on his return.

from **The New Expanded "Forest of Laughter"**,
compiled by You Xi Zhu Ren (The Master of Diversion) and revised by Can Ran Ju Shi (The Merry Hermit) of the late Qing

Justified in the Eyes of the Law

AN official who was thoroughly corrupt and incredibly greedy summoned one day the two opposing parties in a certain case to his office to hear their statements. The plaintiff presented him with fifty taels of silver, but the defendant got wind of this and doubled the amount.

At the hearing, when the official ordered the plaintiff to be summarily flogged, the latter made a hand gesture indicating that he had already paid out fifty taels, pleading: "Obviously my case has merit, Your Honor!" But the official made a gesture of the hand back at him, saying: "Churl! You say your case has merit?" and raising his hand suddenly twice as high, continued: "Well, *his* has *more* merit!"

Cash on Delivery

ONCE an official issued a certificate for the purchase of two gold ingots and the gold shop sent a man with the ingots to him, who was to collect payment on delivery. The official then asked him the price, to be sure, and the man from the shop replied: "Now normally our price for these two ingots would be such-and-such an amount, but for Your Excellency's express purposes, we are prepared to offer a fifty per-cent discount!" The official thought a moment, sized up the situation, and then handed back one of the ingots to the seller.

The gold merchant remained standing there, expecting payment in full for the gold in cash. But the official grumbled: "Well, what are you still standing here for? You can go home now! I've paid you already!" "What?" exclaimed the seller. The official then grew angry and shouted: "Impudent varlet! You stated you would take only half the normal price! Very well, one ingot has been returned to you in lieu of half the price in cash. I've kept my part of the deal! Why stay here and pester me further? Hurry up and get moving! Off with you now!"

A True Likeness?

A portrait painter never got much business until someone advised him to display a portrait of a couple in his shop window to appeal to the newly-wed market. This the painter did, using his own wedding portrait, which he had painted himself, for the advertisement.

One day, his father-in-law came to visit them and,

staring at the picture, asked: "Who is this woman?" "Your daughter," replied the artist. Looking a while longer, the father-in-law stammered: "If that is my daughter, then why have you portrayed her married to someone else?"

A Dead Giveaway

WHEN a portrait was at the point of completion, the artist suggested that his subject show it to some by-standers to determine the degree of likeness. The first person they encountered quickly pointed to the cap and said: "I could recognize you by that!" A second man identified him by his coat, and so on, until finally they approached a third man, and the artist started to coach him, saying: "Others have already identified the cap and the coat in the painting. You, however, are requested to comment upon the likeness of the counte-nance." After much shilly-shallying, the man at length pronounced: "I could tell it was him by the beard!"

A Tender Scalp

AN apprentice barber, causing a number of nicks on the scalp of a lad through faulty manipulation of the razor, became frustrated and wanted an excuse to give up, so he told his master: "This scalp is much too tender for shaving. Perhaps we should wait a while until he has grown up!"

On the Removal of Hair

AS an old man's beard was turning white, he told his concubine to pluck out the intruding hair. But since there was so much of the white already, the concubine merely pulled out the black instead. When the old man went to the mirror he was aghast and reviled the concubine, but she retorted: "How was I to have guessed you wanted me to retain the minority and dispense with the majority?"

A Brown Beard

A man with a brown beard* boasted to his wife: "Men with beards of such light color are rare indeed, stout

---

* The beards of most men in China are black in color. A brown or a red beard is a rarity.

fellows all, who can stand up to any bully." But one day he went out and came back home soon thereafter, beaten to a pulp. The wife then scoffed at him, reminding him of his previous statement about the color of his beard. He then exclaimed: "How was I to know I would meet my match — a man with a red beard appeared today!"

A Dwarf Runs Aground

A dwarf was sailing on a boat that ran aground in shallow water. He tried hard to push the craft off, but fell into the water, which turned out to be over his head. In utter disgust, the dwarf exclaimed: "Great! This *would* happen to *me*! The boat runs aground because the water's too shallow; *I* get out and it's too deep!"

Meat from Sows

A butcher selling a certain grade of pork told his son not to reveal the fact that it all came from sows to customers. Not long thereafter someone came to buy. The son proclaimed: "None of our pork is from sows!" But this made the prospective buyer suspicious and he left forthwith. The father then said: "Son, I already told you to avoid all mention of the fact, so why did you bring it up?" He then started hitting the lad. Soon afterwards, however, another customer came by and, examining the meat, queried: "The skin is very thick; isn't this pork from a sow?" The son snapped back: "Why do you ask? I didn't say anything, did I?"

A Premature Birth

A woman gave birth to a son after carrying him for only seven months. Her husband made inquiries about the matter with practically everyone he met, fearing lest an infant of such premature birth would not survive. One day he brought up the circumstances of the birth to a friend who replied: "'Tis of no great matter. My grandfather was also born prematurely, after having been carried a mere seven months, just as in the case of your son." The father then exclaimed in surprise: "Well, I'd be interested in finding out if your grandfather survived until adulthood or what?"

In Search of Branches

IN the villages they used to saw off tree branches that grew in a "Y" shape and make them into the legs of

stools. When one of the legs of a stool was broken, the
master of a certain house sent his servant to the hills
with an axe to locate a suitable branch. The servant
came back after an entire day empty-handed. In answer
to his master, the servant replied: "Branches in a 'Y'
shape were aplenty, but all of them growing upwards,
and not a one downwards!"

A Duck in the Place of a Goose

A man who was bringing a goose to market set it down
on the ground momentarily, while he went to a public
latrine. During the time he was in the toilet, someone
stole it, leaving a duck in its place. When the would-be
seller returned from the latrine, he was astonished at
what he saw. "How strange," he exclaimed, "that in
so short a time a goose can lose so much weight! It
must be starving."

An Older Woman

THERE once was a man who married an older woman.
Only when looking directly at her as they sat together
on the marital bed did the husband notice that his

bride's face was covered with wrinkles. This prompted him to ask to know her true age. But the wife replied: "Around forty-five." "On the wedding certificate," protested the husband, "you stated your age was thirty-eight. But in my judgment you now seem over 45." "To tell you the truth," replied the woman, "I am 54," consistently maintaining this figure in the course of the endless queries which thereupon ensued.

But after they had gotten in bed, the husband grew even more skeptical and hit on a plan for determining her real age, so he exclaimed: "Wait a minute, I want to get up and see if the salt container has been covered or not, just to make sure the rats don't get in." "Tsk, how ridiculous!" exclaimed his wife. "In all my sixty-eight years, I've never heard of rats eating salt!"

The Demise of Drink

A guest wailed loudly after emptying his cup of grog. "Why be so distressed at the outset of a feast?" queried his host. "Because," replied the guest, "the most important thing in my life has always been drink, but now I wail for its demise!" The host laughed and said: "What do you mean by its 'demise'? Surely no liquor can die!" — "But," responded the guest, "the drinks you serve this night must surely be dead, for they lack even a trace of spirit."

He Called for His Tea

UPON the arrival of a visitor, the master of the house repeatedly reminded his wife that she should be busy preparing some tea. At length the wife responded: "You haven't bought any tea all year. Where do you expect me to get it from now?" "Make some boiled water, then," replied the husband. "Well," she shot back, "we have no firewood either, how can I possibly boil water?"

The husband then resorted to abusive language, saying: "You harlot! You mean to tell me there is no straw in pillows?" But the wife cursed him back, saying: "Tight-wad of a turtle, how can the bricks we always use as pillows be burnt as firewood?"

"Come a Bit Earlier Tomorrow"

SO many creditors gathered at the home of a certain debtor to demand their money back that all the chairs and stools were occupied. One even had to sit on the stoop. The debtor then gave the high sign to him the least fortunate of his guests, and whispered: "Come a bit earlier tomorrow!" The man was pleased as could be that the debtor had singled him out ahead of the others. As he left the premises, he exhorted the others to abandon their cause for the night.

Early the next morning he reappeared at the debtor's house to discuss the secret summons. The debtor then told him: "I felt so sorry yesterday that you had to sit out there on the threshold all day, that I made it a point to get you here earlier today, so you could have a proper seat."

Dream and Reality

A debtor once told his creditor: "I'm afraid I shan't have much longer to live, as I saw my own death last night in a dream!" But the creditor replied: "Remember the principle of *yin* and *yang*! When you dream something, the opposite often takes shape. Such is the principle of duality in the realms of reality and illusion. I have heard that when you dream of death it means you are destined to enjoy a long life!"

"But there was more to it," continued the debtor. "What was that?" queried his creditor. "I dreamt that I repaid all my debts to you first!"

from **The Expanded "Forest of Laughter"**, by Cheng Shijue of the Qing

The Size of the Monkey

A county magistrate had to pay a visit to his superior. After the transaction of their official business was completed, however, he lingered on to engage in casual conversation. At one point his superior spoke, saying: "I have heard that monkeys abound in your county, but, pray, enlighten me as to their size!" The magistrate replied: "The big ones are the size of a large man,"* then realizing he had made a grievous slip of the tongue, he quickly lowered his head in a gesture of deference, adding: "And the smaller ones are the size of my own lowly position."**

Speaking of the Heavens

A group of men were gathered once under a tree, discoursing on the "height" of the sky. The views were

---

* In Chinese the words for "Your Excellency" and "a large man" are homophonous, differentiated only by context and usage. Thus as soon as the words had left his mouth, the county official feared his superior might interpret his meaning in this remark as: "A large one is the size of Your Excellency!" (implying the superior looked like an ape.)

** i.e., office or status in the official hierarchy.

varied and the debate dragged on for a long time without an end in sight. Finally, a villager who was passing by intervened to assure all those present that the "distance between heaven and earth is not more than three to four hundred *li*. A slow ascent might take four days or a speedy one three. But a round trip to and from heaven can take six or seven days at most. Why is this question the cause of such fierce contention?"

Those who had been taking part in the discussion were speechless and asked the villager for the basis of his calculation and system of reckoning. The villager explained: "Don't you remember the custom of bidding farewell to the Kitchen God on the 23rd of the 12th lunar month when he begins the ascent to heaven to present his annual report on the deeds of the household? Well, the Kitchen God is always welcomed back on New Year's Eve — a space of only a week. Hence, a single one-way journey thither can take three, but certainly no more than four days, a distance of roughly three to four hundred *li*.'

At that point, everyone broke into laughter and commended him, saying: "Your explanation is excellent! You are indeed possessed of a gift at discourse!"

Sloth

A woman who was extremely lazy depended on her husband to do everything for her. She knew only to hold forth her arms and wait to be dressed; to open her mouth and wait to be fed. But the occasion arose that the husband had cause to leave town for five days. To make sure she would be fed, he prepared a huge pancake with a big hole in the center, putting it over her head and around her neck. He calculated that the cake would last her five days, and only thus could set his heart at ease as he left. On his return, however, he discovered his wife three days deceased. The cake had been eaten only at the point directly in front of her mouth, where a hole was visible. The rest of it remained entirely untouched.

The Ghost of a Miser

A man followed a life of utter frugality, hardly ever eating and never batting an eyelash at the prospect of starvation. In life, people nicknamed him "that ghost of a miser". One day, while crossing a river, he balked at the idea of paying a ferry fee and chose instead to wade across. But by the time he got to midstream, he was faced with the danger of being drowned and began frantically yelling for help.

One boatman offered to save his life for a token fee of two hundred cash, but that "ghost of a miser" refused, saying: "How about a hundred?" Soon the water reached his shoulders, yet he offered only one hundred and fifty. When the boatman refused, he just sank and drowned.

The miser then became a real ghost and was summoned to the court of the King of Hell who roared: "You ghost of a miser! You always acted as though your money was your life and refused to spend a cent while in the mortal world. Now you are in Hell and will be cast into a cauldron of oil." He heard the roar of the boiling oil and beheld the flames issuing forth from the cauldron with his own eyes, yet the miser began to bargain: "There is too much oil; what a colossal waste! If the cost of the oil were paid to me, I would agree to be roasted without it!"

The underlings of the King then impaled the miser and placed him in the cauldron with a huge iron fork, boiling him into a frazzle, and then escorted his remains back to the palace again. The King of Hell took one look and said: "This man is so despicable that he should be reincarnated as a pig or dog."

The miser replied: "I am prepared to accept such a verdict, but there is one aspect of this judgment which makes me feel unjustly treated." "What?" screamed the King of Hell. "While I was in the mortal world," continued the miser, "I never got to taste scallions. Before changing me into a pig or dog, I should like very much if you were to give me some idea of their flavor."

The King of Hell roared with anger and pointed at him, cursing: "Vile creature! We cannot believe you were so cheap you never bought an onion! And now you want *us* to tell you how they taste. Scallions are sour! Sour, we say! — Not that we get to eat them down here, either, damn you!"

An Offensive Tongue

A man was uncanny in his ability to say the wrong thing at the wrong time to the wrong person. Once when a rich old man had just built a spacious addition onto his house, the man with the offensive tongue went to have a look. Knocking at the gate, he got no response, and so immediately began shouting: "What is this, a door or the gate to a jail? Why is it all locked up like this? I presume its inhabitants have all dropped dead or something!"

The elderly owner came out, mortified to hear such utterances in his new abode and stammered: "I have just spent one thousand pieces of gold to erect this hall — no simple feat. Such inauspicious language is clearly inappropriate and uncalled for here!" But his visitor continued: "If it were for sale, it would fetch only five hundred in return! Why are you demanding such a high price?"

"I am not offering it for sale! What prompts your estimates?" responded the owner.

"It may turn out that I offer good counsel," replied the caller, "for should it burn down you will get nothing in return for your investment!"

Inauspicious Talk

IN another instance, a man begot a son at the age of fifty and many people went to his home to offer congratulations. The man known for his offensive language, of course, wanted to join the group of wellwishers but was advised by a friend to stay away, lest he should say something ill-advised. The man protested: "If I may go with you, I shall not utter a word. Will that do?" Reluctantly, the friend agreed, but only on the condition that he keep silent.

Much to the delight of the friend, he held fast to this vow from the time they entered the feast till the final courses and drinks had all been served.

When they were taking leave of the host, he expressed his thanks and added: "I have stifled myself and kept from uttering a word for my entire length of time here. So should your baby go into convulsions and die of something after I have gone, it will obviously have nothing to do with anything *I* have said!"

Paragons of Self-Discipline

ACCORDING to legend, Che Yin caught fireflies to read by in the darkness, while Sun Kang took advantage of the light reflected from the snow for the same purpose. They were both poor, but eager to acquire knowledge through study.

One fine day Sun Kang went to visit Che Yin, but found the latter out. Inquiring as to his whereabouts, Sun was told: "Yin has gone off to catch more fireflies." Some days later, Che Yin returned the call on a bright afternoon and found Sun standing idle in his courtyard. Puzzled, he asked: "Why are you not reading?" "Because," Sun replied, "judging from the look of the sky today, it seems it's not going to snow."

The Telltale Case

A man secured employment as a servant for the first time, and was still a bit embarrassed about taking on a menial's position. One day his master went out to pay someone a visit and the new servant was required to walk behind him down the street, carrying his master's case. Feeling ashamed at this, he hung a sign from the case saying that he was a luggage salesman. On the street, however, a man yelled for him to come over, indicating that he wanted to buy the case. Pointing to his master in front of him, the servant quickly stammered: "Sorry, it's just been sold to *that* man and I'm on a delivery."

Blind Men's Fish

A group of blind beggars pooled their money to buy fish, but as their coins were few, so were the quantities of fish they could purchase. In the end they decided that since there was not enough to go around, they would place it in a big pot and make soup of it so that each should at least be able to savor the flavor.

Fish was an entirely new food for them, and being unexperienced at its preparation, they put the live ones directly into the pot while still flopping. Some of the smaller ones, however, eluded their grasp and slipped to the ground outside the pot without the knowledge of the blind men, most of whom were already gathered around the pot oohing and ahing in unison: "What superb soup! What overpowering flavor!"

Gradually the small fries on the ground flopped onto the feet of one or two of the blind men, who began shouting: "The fish got out! The fish got out!" At that point, those who had already tasted the soup exclaimed: "Thanks be to Lord Buddha that they jumped out in time! Otherwise the taste would have simply overwhelmed us!"

目　录

历 代 笑 话 选

熊 猫 丛 书

*

《中国文学》杂志社出版

（中国北京百万庄路24号）

中国国际图书贸易总公司发行

（中国国际书店）

外文印刷厂印刷

1986年第1版

编号：（英）2—916—35

00290

10—E—2057 P